"With all my heart, I believe th
see that not only can we thrive ii
every resource we could possibly :
fellow pastor, I've seen the practi... .... take
shape in his life. His message is authentic, and his heart is pure; he desires
to see others come into the same victory he enjoys through real relationship
with Jesus. How he has chosen to respond to setbacks and hard times has
authenticated him as someone who lives out what he teaches. He truly is
a tree planted by the rivers of Living Water bearing fruit in all seasons,
whose leaves never fade, and success attends all he does."

—Amy Tubbs,
Senior Leader, The Way Church, Granbury, Texas

"Steven Walker has taken the fruit of his life and put it into words. The
curious thing to me about anyone who writes a book is whether they write
from themselves or about something they have observed. In *Thrive*, Pastor
Steven Walker has broken the bread of his life and offered it to others to
learn from and grow through. I met Steven as a younger man, searching
for identity and purpose. As his pastor, I have seen a life transformed
into a story that has only begun. I had the privilege of leading Steven to
the Lord and, from that day, he made himself a spiritual son. To many,
loyalty is an aspiration, but to Steven and Holly Walker, it is a way of life.
I am continually inspired by his hunger for the depth of the Word and
his passion to share it with others. Books are a dime a dozen, but stories
transfer inspiration. I have no doubt that as you read this story, it will
transfer to you a desire to have a life worth living, not simply living a life.
You've made a great decision to pick this book up; now follow through
and receive the courage to thrive."

—Barry Tubbs,
Senior Leader, The Way Church, Granbury, Texas

THRIVE

STOP SURVIVING AND START LIVING

STEVEN WALKER

LUCIDBOOKS

Thrive
Stop Surviving and Start Living

eISBN-10: 1-63296-218-7 | eISBN-13: 978-1-63296-218-8
ISBN-10: 1-63296-216-0 | ISBN-13: 978-1-63296-216-4

This book is dedicated to my beautiful wife, Holly.

*Thank you for being my biggest fan, my best friend,
and the love of my life. Without you, this book would not
have been completed. Thank you for joining with me
on this supernatural journey called life.*

And to my son, Landon:

*I love you more than you realize.
May nothing ever convince you that you are anything
less than perfectly made in the image of God.
The world awaits the powerful impact that you will make.*

Table of Contents

Special Thanks ix

Introduction 1

1. Rooted in the River 3
2. Think Like an Evergreen 17
3. Limitless Fruit 31
4. The Starting Place of Growth 45
5. The Journey of Maturity 59
6. Connected Conversation 75
7. Our Daily Diet 89
8. Created to Release 105
9. Inside the Unseen 119
10. When Night Falls 133

Conclusion 147

Notes 149

Special Thanks

Mom

Your Christ-centered upbringing is the reason
I am who I am today. Through the many difficulties
I have brought to you and to me, your love
and support remained unconditional. Thank you for
raising me in the way I should go.

Barry and Amy Tubbs

Thank you so much for believing in me
and sowing in my life.
Your grace-filled leadership and teaching
are the key reasons I am walking
in the supernatural ways of God.

David and Heather Walker

If you had not dragged me to The Way Church
in the middle of my mess, I would not be writing this
today. Thank you for being such a positive influence
and for those deep theological conversations.

Jacob Caselton

Thank you for the many discussions that led to a new understanding of scripture and God's nature.
Through your friendship and teaching,
I have begun the journey of learning
what it means to be in Christ.

My Way Church Family

We wrote this book together. Without the wisdom, correction,
and love from all of you,
this book would be incomplete.

Introduction

I am not a seasoned believer nor am I a theologian. I don't have a Bible degree, and I didn't attend seminary. At first glance, you wouldn't consider me a candidate to write a book, or a Christian book for that matter. Writing was never something I had on my radar, and church was something I did only to keep my mom happy. Yet through all of this, God planned this moment before the foundation of the world. The moment you open this book, you are going on the journey with me.

The wonderful thing about God is that He does whatever He wants, and He uses whomever He wants. As it has often been said, *God doesn't call the qualified, He qualifies the called.* There are many stories in the Bible about unqualified candidates doing mighty things. My story is no different. The things I was afraid of my entire life have become the very things God has anointed me for. It is my belief that the enemy will always attempt to instill fear regarding the abilities God has placed within you. Yet when you discover the Lord's call on your life and fully trust Him, you will step into a destiny that the world will examine and take note of.

In the following pages, I will attempt to show you many things. Some I have learned directly from the Lord, and others mighty men and women of God have revealed to me. Yet in the midst of the massive download that is about to take place, I aim to prove one major thing: *You can thrive in all circumstances.* No matter the season and no matter the time, you were born to stand out for God's kingdom. But this doesn't come without a price. The good news is that Jesus Christ paid the price so every season can be *your* season. No situation becomes too big because the infinite God is on your side and lives within you.

This is not another book with ten steps on how to prosper or a play-by-play on how to be successful. Instead, in the following pages, you will find out who you are and who God is. Yes, there will be practical tips enabling you to walk as a confident Christian and in the fullness of what Jesus paid for. However, at the core of it all, you will discover the beauty of the gospel. There is more to this life than you have been told.

Whether you are a seasoned believer, a new Christian, or someone who is merely interested in Christianity but who has yet to make the jump, this book has something for you. I pray that as you read the next ten chapters, you will fall more in love with God and see Him for who He truly is. For too long, God has been painted as an abusive father, sending hurricanes and raining sickness on people. But this isn't the God I have come to know. He happens to be a good father who wants the abundant life for you. When you see Him in His proper form, everything in your life changes.

There is so much beauty that has yet to be discovered right here in this life. What is seen isn't all there is. You were built with a deep desire to experience the supernatural. It is time to discover what Jesus has made available to all those who call upon His mighty name. No longer will you be moved by the temporal trials that come at you daily. No more will you let others dictate what you do and how you feel. Here is the moment that we draw a line in the sand and forget the past. Now is the time to Thrive!

1

Rooted in the River

We all go through different seasons in life. There are days when we are pumped full of motivation and feel as if we could do absolutely anything we set our minds to. But there are also days when we can barely muster up enough energy and confidence to pull ourselves out of bed to put on a clean shirt. Life for me could best be described as a wooden roller coaster, riding up and down with sharp, bumpy turns, often leaving me in extreme pain. Some seasons of my life have been very green and watered, and others have left me dry and withered.

Ecclesiastes 3:1 tells us that there is "a time for every event under heaven." Our lives are loaded with different times and seasons through which we must learn to walk. The earth itself is even subject to seasons—spring, summer, fall, winter—and we have to adapt to all their different characteristics. We make most of our decisions based on what the weather is like outside. When it's cold, we put on a jacket; if it is raining, we grab an umbrella. However, you won't find me mowing my yard in the winter or lighting up my fireplace in the summer, because naturally, my way of life changes according to the conditions of my environment.

As a Christian, I have found myself in various spiritual seasons of life, some good and some bad. Yet there is one thing I believe God has shown me through all of them. No matter what season of life you may find yourself in, you have the ability to always be green

3

and watered, always bearing fruit. That is a profound statement that I aim to prove in this book. I no longer believe that a son or daughter of God was ever created to live dry and withered—as a disgrace—but rather as a well-watered world-changer. We are actually invited to change our environment rather than succumb to it.

The Bible often compares the Christian man or woman to a tree. Jesus told parables about trees, King David wrote psalms about trees, and King Solomon penned proverbs about trees. One thing I have found is that when God is constantly speaking something over and over again, it means He really wants us to hear it. The wonderful thing about God is that He speaks the same point in many different ways just to make sure we get it.

When you look at trees, you will see that most of them change their appearance based on the current season. Trees grow leaves in springtime and lose them in the fall. Most fruit trees bear their fruit in the summer but are barren in the winter. But what if I told you that a "tree" that belongs to God never has to lose its fruit or give up its leaves? What if I told you that you were born to thrive, regardless of the conditions around you?

The Verse That Changed Everything

I remember one particular day very well. I was praying in the closet of the guest bedroom in my home, and I began seeking God the Father's heart on some things I was attempting to walk through in my life. Although I don't remember exactly what I was experiencing, I can recall that this time in my life wasn't one I could shout about in excitement. As I asked God to speak to me, He took me to these verses, which have become one of my favorite portions of scripture and the foundation for this entire book:

> *Blessed is the man who trusts in the LORD*
> *And whose trust is the LORD.*

4

For he will be like a tree planted by the water,
That extends its roots by a stream
And will not fear when the heat comes;
But its leaves will be green,
And it will not be anxious in a year of drought
Nor cease to yield fruit

—*Jer. 17:7–8*

As I read and reread these verses, I began to receive a new perspective on the Christian life. I knew this was the voice of the Lord. I gained a heavenly perspective that has completely changed the way I think and live. This new way of thinking began to give me hope about my current situation and my future.

The word *stream* in these verses is better translated as *river*. Because this particular tree is planted by the river, its roots reach deep into the waters. Even though the New American Standard Bible is one of my favorite translations, I love how The New Living Translation brings even more clarity to these verses.

But blessed are those who trust in the LORD
and have made the Lord their hope and confidence
They are like trees planted along a riverbank,
with roots that reach deep into the water
Such trees are not bothered by the heat
or worried by long months of drought
Their leaves stay green,
and they never stop producing fruit.

—*Jer. 17:7–8 NLT*

These verses told me that if I am planted by the water, rooted in the river, there is no reason I should ever lose my leaves or fruit. Even though there may be extreme heat all around me, it doesn't affect the source from which I'm nourished. In the natural realm, I base my decisions on the weather around me, but in the spiritual realm, I base my decisions according to where I am planted. If I am rooted in the river, the conditions around me are irrelevant and don't affect my state. When things get heated, it doesn't mean I must wither. The fires of life will not consume me.

Christians are often viewed as a group of individuals who are always in need and are incapable of accomplishing much. I grew up thinking this way. I automatically viewed anyone who had lots of money or possessions or even extreme joy as a greedy person. To me, spirituality was directly connected to how little you had. Although I am not certain where this mindset came from, I vividly remember living very confidently in those convictions.

Somehow, it has become a widespread doctrine that Christians are meant to be poor and powerless because that somehow glorifies God. But my question is this: If God's children look beaten and malnourished, what does that say about His parenting skills? If I brag to all my friends about how good of a father I am yet they look at my son and see him hungry and half dead, they won't take what I say seriously. More than likely, they will call child protective services. But that is exactly how many people view our heavenly father.

That is the doctrine of the devil. He knows we are powerful, and his only hope is to keep us in a place of weakness and ignorance. I believe God wants healthy, whole, and happy children who destroy the enemy's works every day of their lives, who have supernatural contentment in times that demand worry. If Jeremiah 17 is correct, I am rooted in a river that continually nourishes me with the power of life, enabling me to distribute it everywhere I go.

A Season without Rain

I live in the wonderful town of Granbury, Texas, which is home to a beautiful lake. I remember a time several years ago when we went through a very long drought. Rain seemed to be something that only existed in fairy tales, and as you can imagine, the landscape was not something to boast about. Burn bans were in force, plants were dying all around, and our lake got so low that islands began to pop up in the middle. Homeowners were having a hard time selling their lake homes because the lake had dropped 12 feet. Our tourist town became an eyesore, and we were in desperate need of water.

Eventually, after several years of fervent prayers, God brought the rains that filled up our lake and returned our city's natural beauty. Rain was the only substance that could have brought growth back to our community, and it came in abundance.

When we find our spirits in seasons without rain, we have an opportunity to worry. We start making choices based on the weather of our circumstances. But if we believe that our nourishment comes from our roots rather than the rain, we will begin to understand that our lives don't have to submit to external conditions.

> *For he will be like a tree planted by the water,*
> *That extends its roots by a stream*
> *And will not fear when the heat comes;*
> *But its leaves will be green,*
> *And it will not be anxious in a year of drought*
> *Nor cease to yield fruit.*
>
> *—Jer. 17:8*

Being rooted in the river removes any fear we have of withering or drying up. Although my hometown lake dried up due to the weather conditions, the river of God will never dry up. This supernatural water has always been and will always be. Because we are rooted in it, we will never need to fear. The world around us could be as dry as hell, but where we stand is supernaturally soaked.

Don't misunderstand me. I am a firm believer that God does send us rain in seasons and pours out his eternal blessings upon us. James 1:17 says that every good gift and every perfect gift is from above, and Matthew 5:45 tells us that God sends His rain on the righteous and the unrighteous. There are many other verses that speak of the importance and blessings of rain, and I in no way want to diminish that. But I also believe that sometimes we are so busy looking up and asking for blessings, asking for more, that we forget where we are planted and everything to which we already have access.

Make Yourself at Home

Whenever I go to my mom's house for a visit, I have access to everything. She has never yelled at me for drinking the cold water from the fridge or helping myself to some chips from the pantry. That's not because I have a poor understanding of boundaries or believe she owes me something. As a matter of fact, she encourages me to help myself to whatever she has available in her house. It's her nature as a mother. When I am there, I have permission to make myself at home. I never take that privilege for granted. I always ask, and I am always thankful. God has given us access to the kingdom of heaven. He expects us to make ourselves at home and use what is available to us. But all of it is only accessed through faith. Faith is what allows us to experience those heavenly blessings here on earth.

Sometimes, we limit our abilities to what we see in the natural, but we must realize that we pull our resources from the unseen. We are seated with Christ in heavenly places (Eph. 2:6), not one day in the future, but right now on this earth. We belong to a limitless God, and it is time we started living like that. If your natural world is lacking in any area, you must realize that your heavenly father has an ocean of blessings just waiting for you to tap into them. Reach out in faith and take what is in heaven's pantry.

Citizen of Heaven

Let me come at this from another angle and hammer it home even more. As I said before, I live in Granbury, Texas. I am a citizen of that city. With that come certain rights and privileges I take part in. I vote there, and I renew my license there, to name a couple. My city has clothing stores, restaurants, and parks that are easily accessible to me because they are in close proximity. Let's expand further. I am a citizen of the state of Texas. There are exclusive laws there that are different from the rest of the country, and I benefit from them. We have a state flag, state government, and our own tax laws. Let's expand even further. I am also a citizen of the United States of America. I live in a beautiful, free country. I vote for the president, I work at a job, and I can enroll in whatever school I want. My point is, a citizen is entitled to the rights and privileges of their land. I don't mean entitled in a sense that the world owes me something. Rather, I have the ability to access what my country has to offer because I have a legal right.

Philippians 3:20 says we are citizens of heaven. Do you realize what that means? I have legal access to the unlimited resources of heaven's realm. At any moment, I am able to make a withdrawal simply because it is my right as a citizen. What I can see on this earth is not all that is available to me. There have been moments in my life when I actually didn't have the physical resources that I needed. But somehow, some way, exactly what I needed was provided for me. Random people have put money in my hand, unexpected refunds have arrived in the mail, and debts have been canceled supernaturally. God is serious about looking out for those who live in His land.

How can we become citizens of heaven? It is only through Christ who paid the price. American soldiers gave their lives so we could live in a free country. Jesus Christ died so we could live free for eternity.

We could never pay the incredibly high price of belonging to God and becoming a citizen of heaven, but Jesus paid that price for us. Everything heaven has to offer is now accessible to us.

Big Field, Tiny Door

I always thought that the Christian walk could best be described as the game Operation. Remember operating on Sam, picking up the pieces with tweezers and getting zapped if you touched the sides of the openings? I think I have spent a lifetime concentrating on not touching the sides of the path I was on or God might zap me. I believed that my path was a narrow one and that I had absolutely no freedom at all. That belief came partially from my misunderstanding of a particular verse, which resulted in a distorted view of God's nature.

> *Enter through the narrow gate; for the gate is wide and the way is broad that leads to destruction, and there are many who enter through it. For the gate is small and the way is narrow that leads to life, and there are few who find it.*
>
> *—Matt. 7:13–14*

I read these verses and believed my life on earth was a constricted journey down a narrow path with absolutely no freedom. Quite honestly, these verses scared me. But I have found since then that if God's word causes me anxiety, I am more than likely misinterpreting His words of hope. These verses aren't speaking of a narrow walk but rather a narrow gate. What gate is He talking about? How can anyone find it? Jesus explains this and clears this up in John 10:9 where He says, "I am the door; If anyone enters through Me, he will be saved, and will go in and out and find pasture."

Jesus Christ is telling us that He is the door. He is the gate. He is the only way to God the Father, He is the only way to heaven, and in Him we are saved. Our Christian life is not a narrow walk but rather it is entering through a narrow door, Jesus Christ, and discovering a whole new world. Once we walk through that door, we step into a wide-open field and find freedom unlike any we have ever experienced. There is no other way. When we enter through Jesus, we have access to heaven and the abundances within. Heaven isn't just an after-death experience; it is a right-now reality. Jesus tells us in John 10:10 that He came so we can have life abundantly. We are no longer confined to natural limitations because we now reside in a world without walls. You are a mighty tree with roots that run deep into the rivers of heaven. I see the stream in Jeremiah 17 referring to heaven itself and only accessed through Jesus Christ. Those who enter in through Him are always drawing their nourishment from the streams of heaven, allowing us to bear fruit and stay green year-round. A son or daughter of God has no excuse to become withered if he or she remains rooted in the river.

I find it interesting that John 10:9 says that anyone who enters through Christ "will go in and out and find pasture." First, what are we going in and out of? The gate, the door—Jesus. The door separates two realms: heaven and earth. Once we enter through Jesus, we are given access to the kingdom of heaven, but at the same time, we remain present on earth. It is a wonderful paradox to be a citizen of heaven yet a resident of earth. Once salvation occurs, we have the privilege of using natural *and* supernatural resources. Miracles then become common. The word *pasture* in this verse translates to food or nourishment. It means that wherever we go, whether the deepest places of earth or the highest places of heaven, we can continually receive the nutrients needed for supernatural living. I am always being fed, allowing me to thrive in all circumstances.

Abundance Inside and Out

Before we go any further, I would like to establish an important truth that many have gone their entire life without knowing. In John 4, Jesus was having a conversation with a Samaritan woman at a well. At that time, people would go to wells to gather water for their everyday lives. They didn't have the luxury of turning knobs and filling up glasses with temperature-controlled liquid. Instead, they had to journey to the nearest well, fill their containers with as much water as they could carry, and hope to God it was enough.

Jesus started the conversation by asking the woman for a drink of water. She quickly acknowledged the fact that he shouldn't even be speaking with her. She was a Samaritan, and He was a Jew, and apparently these two groups didn't see eye-to-eye. The Bible says that Jews had nothing to do with Samaritans. But Jesus looked past the scandals and racism of the age, saw a daughter of God, and decided to help her. He quickly fired back with this statement:

If you knew the gift of God, and who it is who says to you, "Give Me a drink," you would have asked Him, and He would have given you living water.

—John 4:10

This left the woman very confused. *He doesn't even have a bucket*, she must have thought. *How will he ever get me any water?* She had absolutely no idea what He was talking about, and neither did most of the people Jesus interacted with. He was very good at shifting the thinking of those he encountered.

But Jesus began to explain just what this special water is. He told her that it is a substance that will quench one's thirst better than anything else in this world, how those who drink from it will never thirst again. As He continued, she began to beg Him for this water. She realized that He had something she needed and was fully set on receiving it.

We must understand that Jesus is the source of living water. He is what quenches our thirst, He is what nourishes our hearts, and He is what satisfies our souls. He is the one who gave us life, and in Him, we become a well-watered tree. There is no substitute for this savior. Those who don't know Him miss out on the abundant life they were created to have. You were born to thrive.

So what exactly is this living water that Jesus gives? Jesus made this clear in the following verses:

> "If anyone is thirsty, let him come to Me and drink. He who believes in Me, as the Scripture said, 'From his innermost being will flow rivers of living water.'" But this He spoke of the Spirit, whom those who believed in Him were to receive; for the Spirit was not yet given, because Jesus was not yet glorified.
>
> —John 7:37–39

The Holy Spirit is the living water. We as believers have this very spirit living within us, the same spirit that raised Jesus from the dead. If we have this kind of power, it stands to reason that everything on the outside is puny in comparison to what we carry on the inside. Stop for a moment and think about what this means. God has decided to dwell in you.

In the Old Testament, God dwelt in a temple made by human hands. He instructed Solomon to build Him a temple, or house, that He could dwell in and be among His people (1 Kings 6). It wasn't a tiny little townhouse. It was a multimillion-dollar project that took seven years to build (1 Kings 6:38). It was handcrafted with gold, silver, and precious metals. God didn't want some hole-in-the-wall joint to call His own. He wanted something that would express His abundant nature. God was unable to dwell in humans because they were sinful in nature. It wasn't until Jesus died and rose again that the sin issue was taken care of and we became the righteousness of God in Christ. Thank God we are on this side of the cross! Because of the blood of Jesus, we are now considered righteous, holy, and spotless (Col. 1:22).

In the new covenant, God doesn't dwell in temples made by human hands; He dwells in humans (Acts 7:48). And if the temple that God instructed Solomon to build was worth millions of dollars, what does that say about you? You are worth more than all the gold in the universe. You are priceless. Because the God of abundance decided to make His home in believers, it tells us that we are vessels of abundance. When I actually came to the understanding that God Himself dwells in me, I had the confidence to walk as one without lack, regardless of my external conditions. After all, abundance is first realized on the inside before it is manifested on the outside.

Well-Watered

As a Christian, my ability to stay well-watered is not determined by the rains of the world. If I am always waiting for something to fall down from the heavens, then there will come a time during a desert season that I will become dehydrated. Too often, we expect some external blessing to bring us out of despair and into dancing, but that can never be more than a temporary fix. Stop trusting so highly in your surroundings. They cannot possibly bring you the nutrients you need to thrive. I love what Paul says in 2 Corinthians:

But we have this treasure in earthen vessels, so that the surpassing greatness of the power will be of God and not from ourselves; we are afflicted in every way, but not crushed; perplexed, but not despairing; persecuted, but not forsaken; struck down, but not destroyed; always carrying about in the body the dying of Jesus, so that the life of Jesus also may be manifested in our body. For we who live are constantly being

delivered over to death for Jesus' sake, so that the life of Jesus also may
be manifested in our mortal flesh.

—*2 Cor. 4:7–11*

Notice how he begins by saying that great power is from God and not us. But we partake in this power because of who fills us (the Holy Spirit) and where we are planted. Because of this great power flowing in us and through us, our circumstances don't define our character. When affliction comes, we will not be crushed. When situations try to strike us down, we will not be destroyed. These verses continue to tell us that if we remember the death on the cross, the resurrected life of Jesus manifests within our bodies. When the natural life creates difficult seasons and situations, the supernatural life within us empowers us to produce limitless fruit. Even unto the point of death, we can still thrive. How is that possible? How can I be well-off but have nothing? Because thriving is not just acquiring material possessions, but rather obtaining serenity of heart and mind. It's an inside-out (not outside-in) job. On the flip side, when you become aware of the power within you and the position of your planting, you will begin to transform the world around you. You can't help it. It's just who you are—a world-changer.

What's Next?

Because of the price paid by Jesus Christ, we have been rooted in the rivers of heaven and filled with the living water of the Holy Spirit. We are seated with Christ right now and filled with Him as well. We are in water, and water is in us. If that is truly the case, I can thrive in every season. Although this is an amazing concept, we still find ourselves in dry seasons. Some parts of our lives are nice and nourished, while other parts seem dry and droopy. Whether it be our joy, our motivation, our desires, or our relationships, sometimes it seems these seasons of withering are inevitable. I understand that we experience many painful things that seem impossible to navigate. But I still believe that God has equipped us to stay nourished in all seasons. Just because life around us gets hard doesn't mean we are uprooted from the streams of God's goodness. You were created to thrive. As you read this book, remember that all the principles and ideas are founded upon Jesus Christ. He is the only reason we have the opportunity and ability to live a life of abundance and thrive in all circumstances. Without Him we have nothing, but in Him we have hope. My prayer is that the following chapters give you practical tools and supernatural encouragement to live victoriously as a child of the one true king.

2

Think Like an Evergreen

I definitely do not consider myself an arborist. But I do appreciate beautiful landscaping and love it when my yard is well-kept. Spring is one of my favorite seasons because everything is blooming and I am able to work in my yard. Don't get me wrong, there is beauty to be found in all seasons, but to me, spring holds so much visual value. There is abundant beauty and wonder to witness here on this earth outside the confines of our handmade houses.

But even in the middle of winter, there are green trees. The evergreen tree is a tree that remains green in every season. That is where the name *evergreen* came from. Its leaves do not change their color, and it can withstand even the harshest weather conditions. While other trees and plants are ditching old leaves and gearing up for winter, the evergreen holds its beautiful appearance. It does that by constantly producing chlorophyll, the pigment that allows plants to look green. What a beautiful representation of a child of God. No matter what season of life it is, we stay beautiful. The state of the world around us doesn't affect our ability to thrive.

The Journey Begins

The journey of moving from withered to well-watered begins in our minds. My pastor, Barry Tubbs Jr., once led our church in discovering the importance of our thoughts. He assigned books for us to read and then asked us to write responses. I soon found myself reading other related books in my free time that were not part of the assignment. As I read through each book, I discovered that this principle was rooted in each of them: If you renew your thoughts, you can renew your life. Romans 12:2 tells us to be transformed by the renewing of our mind. If you want to transform the way you live, you must first transform the way you think. You won't be able to live a life inconsistent with your thought life.

Steve Backlund, a pastor at Bethel Church in Redding, California, said something once when he visited our church that rocked my world. He said something like this: We get saved when we believe in Jesus, but we get free when we believe like Jesus. Read that sentence again. That simple statement is packed with power that will completely change your life.

Before you will ever see a change in the way you live your life, you must first begin to change the way you see your life. Your thoughts about yourself are very important because your lifestyle will always reflect your mindset. You will live on the outside what you think and believe on the inside.

That is why it is crucial that we *believe* we are a tree that will never wither. If we refuse to believe we have the ability to stay watered in every season, then it will be impossible for us to live a life that thrives.

Sometimes, what God wants for us is blocked by how we believe. Just because something is God's will doesn't mean it will happen. We have to believe it can happen and believe He wants it to happen. Obviously, some things are nonnegotiable. For instance, Jesus is coming back regardless of what you or I think. God is not taking a poll and waiting for enough responses. That decision is set in stone and will not be moved. But other things are subject to the beliefs and decisions of people. In 2 Peter 3:9, it says, "The Lord is not slow about His promise, as some count slowness, but is patient toward you, not wishing for any to perish but for all to come to repentance." God's will here is that all would be saved, but as we look around at this world, we know that sometimes people don't choose Him.

Just because all Christians have access to an abundant realm doesn't necessarily mean they will step foot in it. The truth is, you can't enjoy what you are unaware of. I may have a sack of cash in my closet, but if I am unaware of its existence, I will never enjoy spending it. We must actually believe in order to benefit.

The Valley of Dry Bones

In Ezekiel 37, God takes the prophet Ezekiel to a valley full of dry human bones. This is not the most pleasant place to be standing, but God brought him there to show him something. The Lord sometimes brings us to an unpleasant place to see if we have faith to transform it. Ray Hughes, founder of Selah ministries, once said that we are sometimes in a desert because God wants to beautify the desert.

God asked Ezekiel, "Can these bones live?" (Ezek. 37:4). I don't believe that God asks us questions because He doesn't have the answers. If that were the case, we serve a very puny god that is only as smart as the ones he creates. But fortunately, that is not the case. God asks us questions to see what *we* will say. It is important to Him that we line up our way of thinking with His.

God is testing the faith of Ezekiel in this passage. He is big enough to do whatever He wants, but He uses His sons and daughters who are like-minded to accomplish His works. God is a master delegator. He lives to empower those He loves. If Ezekiel would have refused to believe life was available in that valley of dry bones, I doubt that this story would have worked out as pleasantly as it did.

Eventually Ezekiel releases a prophetic word that results in every bone coming together to form a great army. What seemed to be dead came to life. That gives us hope knowing that just because something is dry doesn't mean it is dead. It is never too late to revive what appears to be withered.

We must shift our thinking to match how God sees things. The Bible tells us that if we renew our minds, we will be transformed and gain the understanding of God's perfect will (Rom. 12:2). It's not enough to believe *in* God. We must believe *like* God. But in order to believe like God, we must first know how He thinks.

Mind Reader

You may be thinking, *but God's thoughts are unknowable.* Let's take a look. Here is what Paul writes in his first letter to the Corinthians:

> *For who among men knows the thoughts of a man except the spirit of the man which is in him? Even so the thoughts of God no one knows except the Spirit of God. Now we have received, not the spirit of the world, but the Spirit who is from God, so that we may know the things freely given to us by God, which things we also speak, not in words taught by human wisdom, but in those taught by the Spirit, combining spiritual thoughts with spiritual words.*

> *—1 Cor. 2:11–13*

These verses tell us that only a person's spirit has access to the thoughts of the person. For instance, I can't read your thoughts, and you can't read mine. Let's keep it that way. The verses continue and tell us that only the spirit of God understands the thoughts of God. Bummer! If only we could know what God is thinking. But the other verses tell us that we have received the spirit of God—the Holy Spirit. If I have the spirit of God living within me, then I have access to God's thoughts. No longer am I ignorant of how God thinks because I have received the spirit of God—not the spirit of the world. I have the mind of Christ (1 Cor. 2:16). James 1:5 tells us to ask God if we lack wisdom, and He will give generously. Just lift up one sincere question to God, and He will pour out revelation and understanding that give you a glimpse into His mind. He wants to tell you things you have never heard and show you things you have never seen.

A Better Understanding

How we think and what we believe is the starting point for how we live. We must receive heavenly understanding about the world around us and within us if we want to actually have a transformed life. Jesus makes that plain in the book of John:

> *If you continue in My word, then you are truly disciples of Mine; and you will know the truth, and the truth will make you free.*
>
> *—John 8:31–32*

The word *know* in the original Greek language is *ginosko*, which in this context means to be aware of, perceive, or understand. Jesus is saying to His disciples that once you *understand* the truth, then "the truth will make you free." That brings a whole new perspective to those verses. It's not just about the memorization of information but also about whether or not you actually understand what you hear and read.

I remember hating algebra and geometry when I was a teenager. No matter how hard I tried (though I definitely could have tried harder), I couldn't understand what was being taught. That obviously resulted in terrible homework grades and test scores. But somehow I managed to pass those classes. It doesn't matter how many Bible verses we memorize or how many great sermons we hear, our transformed life actually hinges on whether or not we *understand* what we are reading and hearing. The Pharisees in the Bible had great memorization skills and could recite any verse on cue, but remarkably, they missed the very Messiah who was prophesied in those verses.

When you don't take the time to allow the Holy Spirit to bring revelation to the scriptures, you get caught up in all sorts of religious jargon that could have easily been avoided had you not closed your mind to Him. The Bible is written in such a way that makes reading it fully dependent on listening to His voice. Without a Holy Spirit revelation, all we have is a dusty old book, leaving us confused. Revelation is information unlocked by heaven that reveals truths to our spirit as they make their home in who we are. It is the Holy Spirit who reveals what we previously couldn't understand. Revelation is what brings transformation. Once something becomes revelation, we then can release it to others, as we are commissioned to do. As an old saying goes, "You teach what you know but impart who you are."

The more we *understand* what God says, the more transformation we will experience. When we *know* the truth about a certain area of our life, we can walk in freedom in that area. When we *know* the truth about a certain verse, we can apply it to our lives. When we understand God's thoughts about us, it changes our own thoughts about who we are.

The Only Proof Necessary

After being baptized by John the Baptist, Jesus went into the wilderness where He fasted for 40 days and 40 nights. He was sent to a barren land that was absent of life. But He was drawing His life from the spirit within Him rather than the spirit of the world around Him.

At the end of this fast, the Bible says that Jesus became hungry. Notice how it doesn't say that He was thirsty. Maybe that's because He is who the earth thirsts for. The enemy saw an opportunity and capitalized on it. He tempted Jesus with three temptations, hoping to see the son of God fall. My focus here is not necessarily on the temptations but rather what the enemy's temptation language was.

Satan started each temptation by attacking Jesus's belief system, saying, "If you are the Son of God," do this and do that (Matt. 4:3). In other words, "Prove yourself." The only reason Jesus was able to withstand the harsh external conditions and not give in to the devil's game was because inside, He was well-watered with the truth of who He was. He didn't need to prove Himself because He understood that He was already a beloved son in whom God was well-pleased (Matt. 3:17).

God is already pleased with you. You are His beloved, and there is no need to prove that to anyone. When Satan attacks your identity and tests your beliefs, you can boldly declare that the God of the universe loves you.

You Are His Beloved

Growing up, I never really loved who I was. I struggled with depression and hated the person I saw in the mirror. All I wanted was to be like everyone else. I felt as if I could offer the world nothing that it didn't already have and that my best chance of finding happiness was to imitate the idols I created of the people around me. Every time I walked into a room full of people, I automatically expected them to think poorly of me.

My mother always took me to church. Every Sunday morning we would dress up and drive to the church building where we would immediately attend our Sunday school classes, separated by age. After 45 minutes, a bell would ring, and we would join our families in the main auditorium for the service. The problem I had was that sometimes when we arrived for Sunday school, my class door was shut. The last thing I wanted to do was open a door to a class that had already begun. Every eye would be on me. When you hate what you see in the mirror, you expect others to hate what they see as well. So I would go to the bathroom down the hall and hang out in the stall until the bell rang. Then I would find my mother and attend the service with her.

I spent my entire high school years believing everyone was better than I was and that no one liked who I was. I didn't have very many friends because I just assumed they wanted nothing to do with me. I didn't know it then, but I now understand the root of what was going on. The problem was that I didn't know how loved and valuable I was. When someone doesn't truly understand their value, it is impossible for them to love themselves.

I believe that one of the only reasons Jesus was able to withstand the temptations of the enemy was because He received a revelation of how much His heavenly father loved Him. He knew His value. It didn't matter what was said in the wilderness because the words of love from His father played louder in His mind than the lies of the tempter. If I had realized as a teen the love of my heavenly father, I would have been able to love myself. You will never love yourself more than your understanding of God's love for you. As you unravel His love for you, it changes what you see in the mirror.

The Bible also tells us to love our neighbor as we love ourselves (Mark 12:31). That becomes a problem when we hate ourselves. The truth is that it is impossible to love others more than you love yourself. Because I felt the way I did about myself, I couldn't possibly have a healthy perspective of those around me. My relationships were limited due to my distorted view of who I was. If I would have understood the love of God, I would have been able to give the love of God to others. Psalm 139:17–18 says that God's precious thoughts about us outnumber the sands of the sea. God has endless good thoughts about us, so what is keeping us from believing them?

The Mind of Joseph

Most of us remember the story of Joseph. When you were a kid, you probably colored pictures of the beautiful coat his father, Jacob, gave him. I heard it so many times growing up that I thought I knew it well, but it wasn't until recently that the Lord brought revelation that has forever changed the way I see the story.

Jacob was a man who had many sons, including Joseph. The relationship that Jacob and Joseph shared was one-of-a-kind in their family. The story tells us that Jacob loved Joseph more than all his other sons (Gen. 37:3). It obviously didn't please Joseph's brothers that he was getting all the attention, so they plotted to destroy him.

Jacob made Joseph a coat of many colors as a symbol of his love for him. Every time Joseph looked at that gift, he was reminded of the unconditional love his dad had for him. Joseph felt like royalty because it was instilled in him at an early age. Everywhere he went, he must have thought, *I am awesome! My dad loves me! Check out this coat!*

There came a point in Joseph's life when his brothers had had enough of him. They wanted him out of their lives. The first thing they did was strip him of his coat. They took from him the very symbol of love that his father had given him. Satan does the same thing in our lives today. He tries to attack the blessings we receive from God, thinking that it will destroy who we are. But as long as our identity is rooted in the blesser rather than the blessing, we will not crumble.

Eventually, Joseph was sold into slavery and went through a bit of a rough patch. But no matter where he ended up, the Lord made Joseph prosperous. How is that possible? Joseph even ended up in prison, but he found favor with Pharaoh and ultimately became a royal just below Pharaoh himself. That was because Joseph knew, through everything, who he was. He knew his father loved him and that he was a royal son. He eventually was able to live on the outside the way he saw himself on the inside. He never withered according to his surroundings; instead, he transformed his surroundings. The hope within him was greater than the mess around him.

Our God loves us. He has given us a symbol of His love through the death of Jesus on the cross. This is our coat of many colors that Satan can never strip from us. There is no reason we should see ourselves any differently than the way He sees us. We must understand that the river we draw from is a river of love. We are planted in God's never-ending grace, and with it comes abundant joy, abundant peace, abundant love, and abundant life.

A Life of Abundance

Jesus made an amazing statement: "The thief comes only to steal and kill and destroy; I came that they may have life, and have it abundantly" (John 10:10). That verse gives us insight into what God's will is for our lives. If you want to know the nature of God, then look at the life of Jesus. The word *abundantly* in the original Greek language is *perissos*, which means superabundant in quantity or superior in quality. The life Jesus paid for us to live is a life of abundance. There is no reason a Christian should barely be scraping through life hoping he or she makes it to the end of the month.

We were born to thrive. I am not saying that every person will be a millionaire and have everything they ever wanted in the entire world. I am not promoting greed or selfishness. The blessing of the Lord is not to promote selfishness; it is to ignite generosity. Abundance can become an idol if it becomes the thing we seek most. Matthew 6:33 tells us that when we seek His kingdom first, He will provide us with everything else. I am simply saying that we are sons and daughters of a heavenly father who lacks nothing. He is willing and able to meet all our needs and more according to His riches in glory (Phil. 4:19).

God's will is heaven on earth. Our responsibility is to bring the reality of heaven to a withering world. But we will never stand a chance if we, too, are withered. A Christian is a representation of God on this earth. Like it or not, people are drawing their conclusions about God based on what those who claim to love Him look like. If they look at us as people who are lacking, then our God to them will be a god who is lacking. If the unsaved world looks at us and sees a group of half-dead hippies, what does that say about our God? We are not only to believe that God is good, but we are also to show that God is good by how we live and what we say.

Representative

Have you ever had to call customer service because something you purchased wasn't working like you wanted? There have been many instances when I have had to contact companies to settle a shady charge on my bill or complain about faulty service. My hope when calling these places is that they understand my plea and fix whatever I am dealing with. But as you are probably already aware, it's not always a pleasant experience.

Whenever I call customer service, I get many automated choices before I am finally graced with the ability to speak with a person known as a representative. That person's job is to help me to the best of his or her ability while also representing the company he or she works for. Everything that person does or says falls back on the company. My view of this specific company rests in the hands of the representative I am talking to. If I have a bad experience, I will come to the conclusion that the company is no better than the person I spoke with. The opposite is true if I have a good experience.

If my Internet goes out and I call the company, asking them to please fix it, they might send a representative to my house to resolve the issue. He or she shows up at my house, fully decked out in company clothing and a car that has the company's name and logo on it. The experience I have with this person will determine what I think about my Internet provider. If he or she tears holes in my walls, starts a fire in my kitchen, and leaves before I understand what just happened, I will believe the worst about the company. I will also drop their service and tell everyone I know never to use them for their Internet needs. But if the person shows up with a smiling face and fixes my issue with no hassle, I will think highly of the person and the company he or she works for. I will tell everyone I meet about the company's amazing customer service.

We must realize that the world is watching us every second of the day. They are building cases for or against our God based on the way they see us live. They are looking at the way we speak, the way we respond to issues, and the way we treat each other. The world not only needs to hear more good ideas about who God is and what He provides, but they also need to see kingdom truths lived out in the lives of those who say they know Him. It is our heavenly responsibility to represent God in the best way we possibly can. How many more people do you think would be added to the kingdom of God if we actually showed God's goodness instead of just talking about it? Our lives preach louder than our lips. Jesus said to His disciples, "He who has seen Me has seen the Father" (John 14:9). All Christians should be able to confidently make the same statement. We must be willing to demonstrate our doctrine.

When the earth is dying all around, people should be able to look at the children of God and see hope in all circumstances. We should shine the brightest in the darkest places. That is how Paul was able to write a joy book to the Philippians while he was in the harshest prison. The hope in him was greater than the hate around him.

No Longer a Slave

You must see yourself able to thrive and believe that it is God's will for your life before you will actually have sustainable victory in your life. The enemy's biggest weapon against Christians is his ability to trick us into believing that we are something we are not. If he can get us to believe that we are worthless and powerless sinners, we will live a worthless and powerless life.

On January 1, 1863, President Abraham Lincoln issued the Emancipation Proclamation, which stated that "all persons held as slaves" within the rebellious states "shall be then, thenceforward, and forever free."[1] This proclamation held the power to free all African American slaves in the states that were rebelling against the Union. All slaves were legally free to join the war in these specific states and help bring the Civil War to a close. The war had already been going on for about three years up until that point. But it wasn't until January 1, 1865, that Congress passed the 13th Amendment to the U.S. Constitution, which released all slaves nationwide from their shackles to start a brand new life as free citizens.

Slaves were legally free to start over as of January 1, 1863, but as it turns out, they didn't find out right away. Many slaves stayed in their chains under the harsh conditions of their owners because they were never told they were free.

There is a holiday celebrated every year in Texas on June 19 that commemorates the day in 1865—two and a half years after the Emancipation Proclamation—when Major Union General Gordon Granger rode into Galveston, Texas, with 2,000 US troops and announced to the slaves there that they were free. There was nothing anyone could do to stop those slaves from walking away from slavery and to their futures. But why did it take so long? I am among those who believe it was because the slave owners didn't want the slaves to know so they could keep using them as free labor. The slaves had been free for two and a half years but couldn't walk in that freedom because they had no idea they had been set free.

I believe this is exactly what Satan—our enemy—does to us. He knows that Jesus paid the price to set us free, and he knows he has absolutely no power to void it. His only hope is to make us believe we are not actually free and are doomed to stay in bondage. It is time for the body of Christ to stand up and realize we have been freed. The only thing that is keeping you in captivity as a son or daughter of God is what you are believing.

For if we have become united with Him in the likeness of His death, certainly we shall also be in the likeness of His resurrection, knowing this, that our old self was crucified with Him, in order that our body of sin might be done away with, so that we would no longer be slaves to sin; for he who has died is freed from sin.

—*Rom. 6:5–7*

Jesus has freed us from all ties with the enemy. All that is left is for us to actually believe it. The price has been paid, and we are now the righteousness of God in Christ Jesus (2 Cor. 5:21). Romans 6:11 says, "Even so consider yourselves to be dead to sin, but alive to God in Christ Jesus." The key word here is *consider*, which speaks to the mind. In other words, to enjoy this new life, you must believe it to be true. Think free and you will live free. The only captivity that a born-again believer lives in is the cage of his or her own mind.

As you begin to shift your thinking in accordance with the mind of Christ and begin to understand the truth, you are catapulted into freedom, and there is absolutely nothing the enemy can do about it. Understanding brings freedom. The only hope the enemy has is to distort your beliefs and convince you to believe a lie. Underneath every captured Christian is a wrong way of thinking.

Believe that you are the tree that Jeremiah 17 speaks of—that you are rooted in a river that will never run dry. That you will always stay green regardless of the conditions of this world, and that nothing can stop you from bearing the fruit that God created you for. The evergreen never worries about what season the rest of the world is in. It doesn't acknowledge the harsh weather conditions. It knows it was created to stay nourished and naturally beautiful year round. Think like an evergreen.

3

Limitless Fruit

Have you ever walked through a season that was extremely difficult to navigate, a season that seemed to suck every bit of life out of you? If you are over the age of five, I'm sure you have. Hard times creep up on us. One minute everything is perfect, and the next minute a severe storm rolls in that we weren't prepared for. In those times, it's easy to believe we aren't able to produce any type of healthy fruit in our lives, that we aren't able to offer the world anything until we return to sunny skies and smooth sailing. It's in those times that we make excuses for our lack of joy, peace, and love. *I'm just in a fruitless season right now,* we say. I have said this before. But from the moment I read Jeremiah 17, I was forced to change my belief system that supported fruitless seasons.

God has planted you in such a way that you can produce limitless fruit. "It [the tree] will not be anxious in a year of drought nor cease to yield fruit" (Jer. 17:8). A tree planted beside the rivers of heaven continues to receive and give, even in severe weather conditions. The problem is when we take our eyes off the truth and focus on the turmoil. That was Peter's mistake when he was walking on the water in Matthew 14. As long as his eyes were fixed on Jesus, he defied gravity. He was journeying through the earth in a heavenly way. But the second he switched his focal point to the problem, he began to sink into the very thing that was once under his feet. The point is, when Jesus is our focus, nothing can overtake us or overcome us. Sinking into the trials of life is not an option. Whatever is trying to pull you under is actually what Jesus is inviting you to dance on.

The Fig Tree

As a Christian, there is absolutely no excuse for a fruitless season. That may seem like a harsh statement, but let me illustrate my point. There is a unique moment in the life of Jesus that is recorded in two Gospels: Mark and Matthew. Both Gospels give a different account of the same story. Jesus and His disciples were on their way from the town of Bethany to Jerusalem. Along the way, Jesus became hungry and spotted a fig tree in the distance. So He headed toward the tree in hopes of receiving a midday snack. As He approached, He realized that what He thought would feed Him was actually fruitless. The next thing that happened seemed a little out of character for Jesus. Both accounts say that Jesus pronounced a curse on the tree, saying, "May no one ever eat fruit from you again!" (Mark 11:14). Once Jesus spoke those words into the atmosphere, the Bible says the tree withered. Do you think Jesus was having an off day? Was he fed up with the world and His followers and just needed to take it out on something? I highly doubt it. If a barren fig tree caused our Messiah to snap, He probably wasn't a very good savior in the first place. There must be something else going on here.

I am a detail guy. I tend to see the tiny pieces that are often missed when reading scripture. In my studies, I've discovered that Mark added a small detail in his account of this story that Matthew chose to leave out. Before Jesus cursed the fig tree, he stated that "it was not the season for figs" (Mark 11:13). That seems odd. Why would Jesus curse a tree that actually wasn't supposed to be producing? Was He unaware of the times? Did He make a mistake? I don't think so.

Many theologians believe this is actually a symbolic reference to the nation of Israel turning away from God and becoming fruitless.

We find this to be accurate where God speaks of His people in Jeremiah 8:13 and says, "When I would gather them, declares the LORD, there are no grapes on the vine, nor figs on the fig tree; and even the leaves are withered, and what I gave them has passed away from them" (ESV). We see from these verses that God is displeased with Israel's withered, fruitless lives. When we compare the fig tree Jesus encountered and God's message to Israel, we find one common denominator: God likes to see fruit on His trees.

Filled to Produce

God does not expect anything from us that He has not already given us the ability to accomplish. We must understand that we live and operate in a new covenant now. Because of the death and resurrection of Jesus, we now have certain privileges that those before us didn't have. One is the Holy Spirit who dwells in all believers. Because of the Holy Spirit, believers naturally produce certain fruit that comes from within.

But the fruit of the Spirit is love, joy, peace, patience, kindness, goodness, faithfulness, gentleness, self-control; against such things there is no law.

—Gal. 5:22–23

Those who have the spirit of God are able to produce the nine qualities in the above verses, and more. It just comes naturally. Regardless of the circumstances, the fruit of the Spirit comes out. When hate surrounds me, I can release love. When trials attack me, I can experience joy. When life becomes harsh, I can respond with gentleness. God knew that in order for believers to walk in this life, they would be forced to embrace being uncomfortable, that conditions of life would attempt to stress them. That is why we have been given the Holy Spirit. The Bible calls Him the comforter (John 14:25 KJV). We have the comforter to walk through uncomfortable seasons with, and we walk through them without being shaped by them. If the living water—the Holy Spirit—resides within me, every season becomes a fruitful one. I have been filled up to produce out.

Stay Connected

Notice how Galatians 5:22 says "the fruit of the Spirit." That implies that it is actually the Holy Spirit producing the fruit in us and out of us. In John 15, Jesus makes an important revelation to His disciples. It's a revelation that, if correctly understood, would encourage and equip them for the road ahead.

> *I am the true vine, and my Father is the vinedresser. Abide in Me, and I in you. As the branch cannot bear fruit of itself unless it abides in the vine, so neither can you unless you abide in Me. I am the vine, you are the branches; he who abides in Me and I in him, he bears much fruit, for apart from Me you can do nothing.*
>
> *—John 15:1,4–5*

Jesus says we must abide in Him. To abide is to remain. The most important point that Jesus is making in His conversation with His followers is that a connection with Him is vital. He compares God the Father to a gardener, Himself to a vine, and His disciples to a branch. Let's assume that He is referring to a grapevine. As long as we stay connected to Jesus, we grow healthy and produce good fruit. We thrive. Notice how Jesus is comparing us, not to a tree but to a vine. Although they have their similarities, they also have distinct differences. His reason for a vine comparison rather than a tree will become evident in a moment.

When someone is saved, it is because they call upon the name of Jesus and receive His eternal love and forgiveness of their sins. It is then that the entire godhead dwells in that new believer, including the Holy Spirit. If you recall, we learned in Chapter 1 of this book that the Holy Spirit is the living water given by Jesus to every believer to bear fruit and stay nourished. Jesus is making it clear in John 15 that apart from Him, we can produce nothing.

In John 15:6, Jesus gives us insight into what happens when someone does not abide in Him: "If anyone does not abide in Me, he is thrown away as a branch and dries up; and they gather them, and cast them into the fire and they are burned." Here, He is speaking about unbelievers. This verse is not exactly an uplifting verse, yet it is important to understand. Those who choose not to believe in Jesus Christ will miss the heaven created for them and will instead inherit the void of all God's goodness, known as hell.

I don't like talking about hell and Satan because I like to focus on the kingdom of God and spreading the truth of His love. But hell is a reality that cannot be overlooked. That is why it is so important that we use every talent and ability God has given us to model His love and spread His goodness. Romans 2:4 says that God's goodness is meant to lead you to repentance. In other words, seeing how good He truly is sends the world running to Him with a heart filled with love for Him. We were created to experience His goodness. It's a hardwired need within all humankind to know Him and be known by Him. The word *goodness* in the Greek is *chrēstos*, which is actually the root word for *chrēstotēs*, which is translated as *kindness* in Galatians 5:22–23, which speaks of the fruit of the Spirit. Think about that. The Holy Spirit produces out of you the same goodness of God that leads people to Him.

You are a model for His goodness. Fear of hell is a terrible motivator for winning souls, yet many use it. The biblical way to save a soul is to show that person how good God is. Once someone sees Him in that light, they will truly fall in love with Him. God has anointed every believer with specific creativity that He wants released on earth. Be yourself. If you copy someone else, you rob the world of your own earth-shaking creativity. We are not anointed to copy; we are anointed to create. As we live lives of authenticity, releasing our God-given abilities onto this earth, we exude His goodness and attract those who have yet to meet Him.

He Will Lift You Up

The fruit of the Spirit is available to all believers of Jesus Christ. But as you are probably aware, there are times in life that our actions and thoughts don't exactly line up with His list. We act in anger when someone cuts us off in traffic. We let a friend down by not keeping our word. Or we stub our pinky toe on the coffee table and utter words our mothers would not appreciate. Does that mean we don't truly love Jesus? Does this mean we are on a highway to hell and God is displeased with us? The answer is simple. No.

It's easy to look at the lack of fruit in our lives and become discouraged. It's wonderful that the Holy Spirit produces fruit within us, but how is that practically lived out day by day? How do I actually keep fruit on my branch? Let's look at what Jesus says.

Every branch in Me that does not bear fruit, He takes away; and every branch that bears fruit, He prunes it so that it may bear more fruit.

—John 15:2

Here, Jesus is talking about two types of people: those with fruit and those without. Notice how He begins by saying "every branch *in Me*"? That implies that He is speaking about believers, not unbelievers. Whether we are bearing fruit or not, the final outcome Jesus longs for is that we may *bear more fruit.* Let's dig into the first half of this commonly misunderstood verse.

There are two words in that verse that once instilled much fear in me. But I believe it was because I had not personally unlocked the true understanding of what Jesus was saying. Those two words are *takes away.* What did He mean by that? Earlier He called me a branch. As a child of God, if I am not bearing proper fruit, is Jesus

36

going to throw me away to be burned? Is He going to curse me like He did the fig tree and leave me withered and useless? Absolutely not!

The Greek word that is translated *takes away* in this verse is *airō*, which also means *to lift up*. With that bit of information in mind, let's look at that verse again. "Every branch in Me that does not bear fruit, He [*lifts up*]" (John 15:2). This small change completely shifts our understanding of Jesus's words. Jesus is not saying He will kick us to the curb. He's telling us that if any child of God is lacking fruit, He will lift them up to produce properly. That's a major reason He is comparing us to a grape vine rather than a tree. Grape vines need the support of a sturdy structure such as a fence line or a pole in order to climb and produce. The vine is actually being lifted up. If the vine can't climb, it is not going to produce properly. But a good vinedresser will lift up the low branches and tie them onto the structure.

Tucked away within this is the secret of bearing fruit when we seem to be barren. That secret is God Himself. Through Him we produce limitless fruit. Paul understood this same revelation when he wrote:

> *I know how to get along with humble means, and I also know how to live in prosperity; in any and every circumstance I have learned the secret of being filled and going hungry, both of having abundance and suffering need. I can do all things through Him who strengthens me.*
>
> —*Phil. 4:12–13*

Through God, we produce regardless of circumstances. When life pushes us down and demands withering, God the Father (the vinedresser) pulls us up, allowing Jesus (the vine) to nourish us with the Holy Spirit (the living water), which empowers us (the branches) to bear fruit endlessly. What a beautiful picture of the trinity working together in our lives.

Pruning

John 15:2 also speaks to those of us who can see fruit hanging from our lives: "Every branch that bears fruit, He prunes it so that it may bear more fruit." Instead of letting us off the hook and telling us we did a good job, Jesus says He will prune those who are already producing. Why does He do that? When gardeners prune vines, they remove certain limbs and leaves. When they do that, the vine is actually able to produce more fruit. When you cut back some of the limbs, the vine becomes healthier. It does not have to waste precious nutrients to fuel less productive limbs. When a vine is left alone and not cared for, many branches grow that waste the vine's resources, stifling the amount of mature fruit produced. But when those little limbs are pruned, the branch produces more. God wants us as Christians to produce as much mature fruit as physically possible. A vine left to itself to grow wild is not His will. He wants to prune us, to shape us.

This begs the question: How does He prune us? Jesus continues in John 15:3, "You are already clean because of the word which I have spoken to you." He prunes us through His word. Everything Jesus had said to His disciples up to that point was to cut away lies and wrong beliefs. As the Lord speaks to us, He prunes us. The enemy often comes in our lives with false ideas and bad theology in an effort to waste our resources. But as we listen to the voice of God through His written and spoken word, He reminds us of truth, ultimately snipping off the enemy's limbs. Our vinedresser is constantly shaping us and lifting us up in His strength to produce what our true nature was created to release. Every time the enemy attempts to deceive you with a lie, God is waiting with His pruning shears.

Shifting Your Focus

There are many self-help and Christian-living books, including the one in your hand, that try to help people be the best person they can possibly be. They provide practical tools that are created to equip the reader with joy, peace, patience, and many other qualities listed in Galatians 5. While these are sometimes helpful, at the end of the day, the true and only way to have sustained fruit in our life is to stay connected to the source of life. Let Him lift you up. Fruit doesn't come from external sources. It comes from within, from who we are, as the living water nourishes us and allows us to bear fruit. We do not have to focus on the fruit.

I have a peach tree in my backyard, and every year it produces peaches. I have never seen an apple or an orange on it. It always, 100 percent of the time, produces peaches. Interestingly, that peach tree doesn't have to worry about what type of fruit it will produce. All it has to do is receive nutrients and stay well watered. It's not left alone sitting in my backyard day and night, doing everything in its power not to create an apple. It simply remains planted, drinks water, and creates what it was born for.

The problem we often face is that we are trying too hard to produce fruit. We are reading all we can about what to do, continually focusing on the fruit. When your focus is the fruit, you stop paying attention to the water source. Jesus said He wants to help you produce what will come naturally. He is our source of living water. He wants to properly nourish us. When our eyes are fixed on God, everything in our life begins to reflect His perfect nature. As we behold Him, we begin to live like He lives. If I wake up every morning connected to Jesus, then concentrating on the fruit of my life is pointless. Fruit is a byproduct of connection. When I discover my connection, I will see a change in my thoughts and actions in a positive way because my eyes are pointed in the right direction. It sounds so simple, but the most simple is often the most impactful. Too many people are striving to get what the Holy Spirit wants to produce naturally.

It is common today to run to various external sources to give us the fruit our lives long for. If we need joy, we watch funny videos; if we need peace, we soak in calming worship music. There are even times after a long day when we run home to enjoy some comfort food in hopes that contentment will return. While this approach will bring comfort in the moment, it soon vanishes, returning us to where we left off, creating an addiction to the very thing that gave us temporary fulfillment. God has ordered our lives, not to get energy from the things around us, but to be fueled by the power within us.

Continually going to external sources to grow our fruit is like duct taping a peach to an apple tree and calling it good. We have the wonderful ability to allow the spirit of God to produce His fruit from within us. Although watching a comedy for joy or soaking in sweet music for peace is beneficial, allowing God to bubble up joy and peace from within us, through intimacy and connection, is the only way to keep bearing fruit in all seasons. I am not forced to try harder to produce. I am simply invited to drink from Him. He feeds me everything I need, and before I know it, I am filled with peace, joy, patience, and much more.

The Good Tree

Many believers walk through life believing the worst about themselves. They struggle with thoughts of inadequacy and hopelessness that keep them from living victorious lives. In the previous chapter, we learned the importance of our thoughts and beliefs. Because of wrong mindsets, many people think of themselves as a bad person or a bad tree. Maybe they did something in the past for which they can't seem to forgive themselves, or maybe they are convinced that both good and bad live within them, and that the conflict will only be resolved when Jesus comes back to take us home. Either way, anything less than understanding your true nature and identity is unhealthy.

Jesus gets rid of this negative perspective with these words:

So every good tree bears good fruit, but the bad tree bears bad fruit. A good tree cannot produce bad fruit, nor can a bad tree produce good fruit.

—Matt. 7:17–18

This is such a powerful, freeing statement—and many have missed it. Did you catch it? Jesus is saying that a good tree *cannot* produce bad fruit. It's impossible. Good trees can only produce good fruit. The focus in this verse is actually not the fruit but rather the nature of the tree. Jesus brings everything down to a simple example and states the obvious. Good trees can only produce good fruit, and bad trees can only produce bad fruit. With that understanding, the obvious question is this: How do I become a good tree?

The only possible way to become a good tree is to die. I don't mean physically; I mean spiritually. We were born into this world as sinners, as bad trees. That is why Jesus tells us that "unless one is born of water and the Spirit he cannot enter into the kingdom of God" (John 3:5). *Born of water* refers to natural birth when the mother's water breaks. *Born of the Spirit* refers to the rebirth that takes place when salvation occurs in someone's life. Their spirit is reborn and completely recreated; the old is dead, and the new is born (2 Cor. 5:17).

You see, when Jesus died on the cross, we died with Him. We have been crucified with Christ (Gal. 2:20). When someone truly accepts and believes in Jesus, they become a good tree in the blink of an eye. From then on, they are incapable of producing bad fruit from within themselves. How is that possible? Because with a new spirit comes a new nature, a perfect God-like nature that produces only good. Jesus said, "Make a tree good and its fruit will be good, or make a tree bad and its fruit will be bad, for a tree is recognized by its fruit" (Matt. 12:33 NIV). Salvation actually enables a life change. God didn't change our fruit from bad to good. He uprooted the old diseased tree and planted a brand spanking new one.

What's with the Bad Fruit?

Even though this is true and amazing, sometimes it seems like we see bad fruit on good trees. How is that possible? Because of this perceived contradiction, many create excuses for bad fruit and just believe that's the way it's supposed to be—that Christians will always struggle with proper production, that we will be hosting good and bad fruit on our trees until the sweet embrace of death. To believe this way is to say that Jesus didn't do a good enough job on the cross. That is obviously not true. But the question remains: Why do we find bad fruit on good trees? We know now that according to Jesus, a good tree only produces good fruit. Let's call that fruit *edible*. And we know that a bad tree produces bad fruit. Let's call that fruit *poisonous*. Now we have two completely different trees with completely different fruit.

The peach tree in my backyard only produces peaches. I consider it a good tree with edible fruit. It is impossible for that tree to ever produce poisonous fruit. Within its DNA is only the ability to produce peaches. Even so, on different occasions I have found rotten fruit hanging from it. When the peaches are rotten, they are no longer edible. But rotten fruit is not the same as poisonous fruit. Do I blame the tree for what is rotten? Do I assume that this disgusting harvest came from within it? Absolutely not! I know that something external has come and corrupted what was once edible.

The bad fruit that is seen in the believer's life is not poisonous; it is rotten. There is a major difference. It is impossible for it to be poisonous if the tree is good. You must understand that the believer cannot produce evil from who they truly are. What is actually happening is that they are being influenced by an external source, causing the good to rot. That changes everything. We don't have to try to change who we are. That was done when we said yes to Jesus. We have been made righteous and spotless (Col. 1:22). When we are negatively influenced in this life, all we can do is allow God to remove what is no longer edible. Allow the words of His voice to prune all fruit that has been externally corrupted. Don't question the source of the produce. Allow God to reveal what has influenced it. A tree may be recognized by its fruit, but it is not defined by it. I am defined by what He did. The state of the fruit in your life only reveals what is influencing you.

What Are You Letting In?

We all have the potential to be influenced by many things in our lives. Movies, music, family, friends, and co-workers are just a few of the countless outside sources that can impact us. Because of this, we must always be mindful of what we are allowing into our lives. Whether we realize it or not, the things we are continually watching, experiencing, and listening to are shaping what we believe and how we see the world around us. These sources can be good, but some of them can also be poisonous and hazardous to the lives of believers. It does not affect who we *are*; it affects who we *think* we are. As reborn children of God, the fruit of our lives is always pure; that is, until it encounters the influence of poison.

In Matthew 16, Jesus tells His disciples to beware of the leaven of the Pharisees. Leaven, or yeast, is added to dough to make it rise. Think of it this way. Leaven changes the state of the dough. In this context, Jesus is using leaven as a metaphor for negative influence. Let's consider the leaven in this example as poison. Jesus is sternly warning His followers not to allow the wrong things to influence them. Paul, in 1 Corinthians 5:6, tells his readers that a little leaven affects the entire lump of dough. He continues in verse 7, "Clean out the old leaven so that you may be a new lump, just as you are in fact unleavened." I love how the New Living Translation says it: "Then you will be like a fresh batch of dough made without yeast, *which is what you really are*" (emphasis added). Paul is saying that your true nature is actually already unleavened—uncorrupted. Who you truly are is righteous, and there is no leaven found on the inside. While the leaven of life can't change your new nature, it can certainly change the state of what you produce.

43

I remember a time in my life when I had a close friendship with someone I worked with. I was just beginning the journey of discovering the beauty of the kingdom of God and was learning all I could. During that time, I was easily influenced by pretty much anything. I failed to see the importance of guarding myself from negative influences. As it turns out, this person became a huge hindrance in my life, so much so that it negatively influenced the way I lived and thought. I was blinded to the leaven of this particular person, and because of that, the fruit of my life was corrupted. I eventually broke off the relationship and was able to return to living like who I truly was.

We must protect ourselves from negative influences. I am not saying that we should build walls of fear that shield us from life itself. All I am saying is that we should watch what we allow into our lives. When I allow external poison to influence the pure produce of my life, I am left with rotten fruit hanging from my tree. Remember, it didn't come from the inside. It was influenced by what I allowed into my life. What are you letting in? What are you allowing to influence you? Don't let anything change the state of the fruit of your life.

Limitless Fruit

You are fully capable of producing limitless, pure fruit, regardless of the season of life you are in. Even though you may be in a season that should naturally be barren of joy, Jesus has provided you with the ability to produce. You are connected to Him. As a matter of fact, you are one with Him (1 Cor. 6:17). As you live your life, God produces His fruit out of you. Striving to release what you can naturally produce is a waste of time—time you could spend enjoying the effortless life with Christ. In the end, your striving doesn't help you one bit. You are the good tree that you are, not because you strived but because He died. Stay connected to Him and be yourself—your spotless, blameless self.

4

The Starting Place of Growth

When I was a child, I shared a room with my younger brother, and as you can imagine, we had our share of arguments. Most of them were about each other's belongings. I look back in amazement at how my parents never threw in the towel and skipped town. My brother and I both had our own toys, but the problem was that they were all mixed together in the same room. I would come in our room at various times throughout the day and find him playing with my toys. "That's mine!" I would shout. "Get your own!" While this statement was probably rooted in selfishness, there is still an important thing to realize.

When someone uses something that belongs to someone else, they are always subject to the owner. They need permission from the owner and must work around the convenience of the one to whom the shiny toy belongs. I may have the ability to use my neighbor's pool, but there are certain restrictions put on me. That is how a lot of people view God. They don't realize that they were created to enjoy their own relationship with Him, and instead, they spend their lives following other people around, hoping they can drink up some of the God they so desperately long for. We must realize that a personal relationship with God is what enables us to thrive in this life. Failure to do so will result in our missing out on the true beauty of our created purpose. God is inviting each of us into intimacy with Him. The starting place of all growth is realizing your personal connection with God. A tree is rooted in something. What it is rooted in determines the tree's vitality. You happen to be rooted in God.

A Testimony That Brought Transformation

Let's go back to Jesus talking with the Samaritan woman at the well in John 4. When they finished the conversation, she ran back to her hometown and told everyone of her encounter. She was so excited that she left her water jar behind. It was the very thing she had left her house to fill. Instead, she was filled with hope. Isn't it funny how our plans change once we have a conversation with God? We end up leaving behind what we thought was so important. This woman told her entire village of her encounter with Christ, and many of her fellow Samaritans believed in Jesus.

It is interesting to me that they believed in someone they had never met. Apparently, this woman's testimony was so convincing that it shifted the hearts of the people. She had a life-changing encounter with God in the flesh and brought it back to where she lived. That is a beautiful picture of evangelism. We have daily opportunities to tell those in our lives about the one who won our hearts, ultimately resulting in a chance for their salvation.

But the Samaritans didn't stop with the woman's testimony. They didn't want to rely on her words to keep them believing for the rest of their lives. Instead, it compelled them to meet this Jesus for themselves. Our encounter leads others to their own encounters. With every testimony we tell, we give the hearers an opportunity to receive their own testimony. When someone shares a testimony, the power of God that originally produced it is released into the atmosphere, creating the possibility to reproduce it.

The Bible says that those who heard the Samaritan woman's testimony went to Jesus and asked Him to stay with them, which

He did for two days. They went from hearing about Him from a friend to seeing Him as a friend.

Many more believed because of His word; and they were saying to the woman, "It is no longer because of what you said that we believe, for we have heard for ourselves and know that this One is indeed the Savior of the world."

—John 4:41–42

These Samaritans may have started with someone else's testimony, but it eventually led them to their own personal conversation with Jesus. We can only last so long riding on the coattails of others before we need to see our Lord face-to-face. If we think we have a relationship with God through another person, we will dry up in seasons when we are not with them.

God doesn't want to know you through your parents or your friends. He doesn't want to know you through pastors or prophets. Since the beginning of creation, all God has longed for is to have a personal, intimate relationship with each one of his beloved children. That is the only reason He sent Jesus to die for us. Sin had separated us from experiencing perfect love, but God made a way. We are once again invited to live with Him.

Many Christians in the world think that only pastors and preachers can know God and have a close relationship with Him. But what they fail to realize is that we were all created for a relationship with Him. We have all been given access to Him through the cross. The blood of Jesus gave us the right to stand before Him unashamed and unafraid.

Fear Not

When the Israelites were roaming in the driest places of the desert, they were being led by a man of God named Moses. Every day,

Moses spoke with God and then told the people about the conversations. That allowed the Israelites to have a relationship with God through another person—Moses. Whenever I have a relationship with someone through someone else, I never see that person correctly. It becomes a completely withered relationship. I find myself drawing good and bad conclusions about who the person is, even though I have never met them. Honestly, the worst way to know someone is through someone else.

That was the Israelites' problem. They saw the mighty works of God but never actually established a personal relationship with Him. There is an interesting passage in Exodus 20 that gives us a glimpse of why that was.

All the people perceived the thunder and the lightning flashes and the sound of the trumpet and the mountain smoking; and when the people saw it, they trembled and stood at a distance. Then they said to Moses, "Speak to us yourself and we will listen; but let not God speak to us, or we will die." Moses said to the people, "Do not be afraid; for God has come in order to test you, and in order that the fear of Him may remain with you, so that you may not sin." So the people stood at a distance, while Moses approached the thick cloud where God was.

—Exod. 20:18–21

The Israelites wanted nothing to do with this God because they were afraid of Him. They distanced themselves and asked Moses to only let them know what He said. Their fear of God pushed them away from Him. Many of us hold fast to this same mindset today. We are afraid to get close to Him, so we stand back at a distance and ask the pastors to tell us what He says. This type of fear is extremely unhealthy for a child of God.

Moses told the people to not fear because God wants the fear of Him to remain in them. What? Are you confused yet? But under what looks like a contradiction is a distinction between two types of fear. Any fear that pushes you from God instead of pulling you to God is a corruption from the enemy. The Bible is full of verses that tell us to fear the Lord, but this fear is not what sends us running in the opposite direction of His open arms. The first fear mentioned in Exodus 20:20 is *yare*. That is the same Hebrew word used to describe the fear Adam and Eve felt in the garden after they ate of the forbidden fruit and hid themselves. This fear sent them running away from the God who once freely walked with them. The second fear mentioned is the Hebrew word *yir'ah*. Throughout the book of Proverbs, King Solomon used this word for fear to describe the fear of the Lord. In Proverbs 1:7, he stated that the fear (*yir'ah*) of the Lord is the beginning of knowledge. That sounds like the fear of the Lord all believers need.

I believe that we can glean this important truth from what Moses was saying to the people of Israel. Don't allow the fear that keeps you from God to replace the fear that uncovers the need for God. When we understand God's love for us, it is perfected within us and removes all unnecessary fear (1 John 4:18). A son or daughter of the king doesn't need to hide in fear. Instead, we have the right to boldly approach the throne and crawl right up into His lap.

The Power of Making God Personal

When Moses went up the mountain to receive the instructions of the Lord, the Israelites didn't go with him. Instead, they stayed below waiting for this holy man to return with directions on what to do and where to go next. When Moses left the Israelites, so did the presence of God. They could only witness His presence as long as Moses was in close proximity. Today, that is not the case. Every Christian carries God's presence with them everywhere they go (1 Cor. 3:16). That is what brings heaven to earth, when the people of God release the power of God because they are carrying the presence of God. You carry the kingdom of God within you and have the ability to release it wherever your feet tread. God no longer dwells in temples made by human hands. He dwells *in* people. You are a temple of God (1 Cor. 3:16). The old covenant was God externally, but the new covenant is God internally. That is what allows all sons and daughters of God the ability to change any atmosphere simply by stepping into it. Where you go, God goes.

Moses was on the mountain for 40 days and 40 nights. That left the Israelites without God for that long as well. They finally came to the conclusion that they needed a new god since Moses was showing no signs of returning. When there is a God-void, it will always be filled with something, whether it is with God or a god we create. I will go deeper into that idea in Chapter 8. It is absolutely necessary that we see God as personal. We can't expect to stay well-watered in all seasons if our time with God is dependent on someone else. He wants intimacy. He wants that one-on-one connection that requires both sides to contribute. As we draw close to Him, He, in turn, draws close to us (James 4:8). It's not a matter of becoming physically closer together. After all, He is already in you. Instead, I am speaking of a mental shift that recognizes how accessible He truly is.

God doesn't want to be rented out to the world. He doesn't want to be treated like a movie at Redbox or a vacation house at the coast. He wants us with Him every second of the day, walking and talking together just as Jesus modeled for us. The reason Jesus was able to say that He only did what He saw God the Father doing was because He actually cultivated a lifestyle of intimacy with God (John 5:19). Too often what we do is dress up to go see Him on Sundays while we spend the rest of the week away from Him and think that will suffice. We end up robbing ourselves of experiencing our beautiful connection. The Christian life is not a weekend event;

it is a lifetime commitment. There is absolutely no substitute for a personal relationship with God.

Supplement vs. Substitute

Jude Fouquier, pastor of the City Church in Ventura, California, once said something like this at a conference I attended, "What God grants as a supplement, He will curse as a substitute." Think about what a supplement is. It is a collection of necessary vitamins and minerals, usually in pill form, that helps people stay healthy. It doesn't replace your daily diet; it merely adds an extra kick so you stay in the best shape. I take some occasionally. My bottle says on the side to take with food. If I do that, then life is good. But if I stop eating real food and only take the pills, eventually I would probably wither up and die. Why? Because supplements were never created to be a substitute for real food.

There are many things we have been given to supplement our spiritual diet. Sermons, books, podcasts, and songs are just a few examples. These things are absolutely amazing, and I encourage all believers to add them to their daily diets. The problem arises when these supplements start substituting for God. Resources about God were never meant to replace intimacy with God.

In my short time in ministry, I have heard a certain phrase from churchgoers more times than I wish. They say something like this: *This church just isn't feeding me enough.* Here is what they are really saying: *Someone else is responsible for feeding me truth because I can't do it myself, yet they are feeding me things I don't like.* You and I are responsible for tending to our own spiritual needs. You will never get from a sermon what you will get from intimacy with God. Too many people treat the church like a restaurant. They receive their meal made from the hands of another only to send it back with a complaint to the chef while demanding a refund and declaring they will never be back. Then, they give it terrible ratings online so others can save themselves the hassle of what they went through as they continue the search to find that perfect place to eat. Maybe that's why they are called church*goers*. Because they *go* from church to church, never allowing enough time to get connected and actually give something. Food tastes better when you make it yourself. My pastor often says something like this: "All a sermon is, is just someone else's regurgitated food."

There is no substitute for intimacy with God. Even this book will never give you the ability to thrive in all circumstances. At best, it will buy you a couple of months before you spiral into your next dark season. God is the only one who will give us the resources we need to stay well-fed and well-nourished. My hope is that this book doesn't replace Him but instead gives you an appetizer that gets you started as God brings you into the kitchen to prepare your meal. The keys to heaven's secrets lie behind the door of intimacy.

Rooted in the Word

There are many books about God that are absolutely amazing. I love books and am constantly adding more and more to my reading collection. Even so, no matter the amazing wisdom that is written on each page, no book will ever replace the Bible. The Bible is the written word of God consisting of 66 books, written by 40 authors making it, in my opinion, the greatest book of all time. It is God's love story to us. As we read each page, we discover His nature and uncover His heart. We encounter daily trials and troubles that have the potential to challenge and change current beliefs. Those who stay rooted in the word have the ability to always line up their beliefs with His truths rather than adjusting them according to their current problems.

It is impossible to stay fresh with new God encounters apart from His word. It will keep you flourishing in all seasons. Sometimes, all you need in the moment is one good verse that will take you from down in the dumps to high on a hill. Many of us find ourselves in dry seasons simply because we have traded the word of God for people's words about God.

Many of the answers we seek in life can be found right on the pages of the book some of us haven't opened in a while. Too often we run straight to a pastor, a friend, or Google instead of diving into the sea of revelation that is right under our noses. There is absolutely no excuse for people not to be reading the Bible. Even if you don't own one with pages, you have one available on your phone or computer at all times. Maybe the reason you haven't received an answer from God is because He has already answered it in His word. Why would God speak something new to a person who has expressed absolutely no interest in what He has already said? This is not to bring condemnation to anyone but rather to awaken you to the beauty of the Bible.

Every time we read a chapter or a verse, there is the opportunity to see life differently. This resource is so packed with truth and life that it sends you higher and higher up the ladder of understanding and allows you to gain heaven's perspective of the world around you. You begin to see your problems differently. Your mind becomes renewed according to how God thinks.

No matter how many times we read a verse, we can always gain something new from it. It is unwise to come to a place where you think you have a verse all figured out. The verses that we think we completely understand are actually eternal wells from which we can continually draw. Each verse is so multifaceted that every time you read it, you see a new side of what you thought you knew already. Even if it isn't necessarily new information, it could be the very thing your soul needed to hear at that moment.

Eyes to See

One of the comments I often hear atheists make is that there are contradictions in the Bible. They use this in debates and believe that just because they don't understand something, it automatically means it's not true. I wish this way of thinking had worked in geometry class. I believe God intentionally put what some view as contradictions in His book to keep us digging, to let us know that we don't actually have everything figured out yet. I understand that sometimes there are contradictions in translations and that sometimes details don't line up, but these are very small issues that can usually be resolved. I am talking about verses that seem to say the complete opposite of what another verse says. I will give you an example.

In John 10:10 it says, "The thief comes only to steal and kill and destroy; I [Jesus] came that they may have life, and have it abundantly." That is one of those coffee cup verses that everyone loves and can shout about in excitement. Obviously, it is a glimpse into God's will for His children. But then we come to Matthew 19:24, which says, "It is easier for a camel to go through the eye of a needle, than for a rich man to enter the kingdom of God." There are many views on what "camel to go through the eye of a needle" means, but I think we can all agree that He is emphasizing the difficulties that come with being rich. But how can that be? I thought He wanted the abundant life for me. These two verses don't line up, so none of it must be true, right?

But don't ditch the entire Bible too quickly. Behind this complication is a revelation of kingdom living. If we apply both of these verses to our lives, it will allow us a life of abundance without making money or possessions our god. The rich young ruler to whom Jesus was talking in Matthew 19 had made his possessions his god. Jesus knew that and gave him what he needed in that moment, even though it was difficult for him to hear.

The word is full of many complicated verses that seem to contradict each other, but they actually contain revelations for kingdom living. Get excited when something in the word doesn't seem to line up, because on the other side is a new lens for viewing life. Behind every complication there is a revelation. Hebrews 4:12 says:

> *For the word of God is living and active and sharper than any two-edged sword, and piercing as far as the division of soul and spirit, of both joints and marrow, and able to judge the thoughts and intentions of the heart.*

This is the pruning process that we looked at in Chapter 3. As we stay in His word, the word begins to cut away wrong mindsets and thought patterns. We have all had moments when we thought we were doing something right, only to find out, while reading the word, that God has a better way. As we read the hard verses, He begins to prune those thoughts that do not need to exist in the mind of a child of God. If we only read the easy verses and choose to run from the ones that sting, we can begin to develop things such as greed, hate, and jealousy. When your mind gets offended by the Word, it is because God is trying to reveal something to your heart.

There is no substitute for a personal study of the Bible. It is an essential element of the Christian life, and every believer should dive into the Bible daily. Books are great, but there is only one book that can reveal the perfect will and nature of God. The only reason we are called to read the Bible is to grow in our knowledge of who God is and who we are. If you are not more in love with God after a personal study session, then you have missed the point of His words. Stay rooted in the word, for it is a key to thriving in all seasons.

The Blesser

Having a personal relationship with God allows us to tap into heaven's well at any time and pull out the things necessary for living supernaturally. We have complete access to the giver of all good things, and He wants to meet with you. He wants to bless you. But if we keep ourselves mentally distanced from Him, we will never get close enough to receive the gifts He freely gives us. James 1:17 says, "Every good gift and every perfect gift is from above, coming down from the Father of lights, with whom there is no variation or shadow due to change" (ESV). Our blessing is contingent upon our intimacy with Him.

Sadly, many people want the gift without a relationship with the giver. This is nothing more than treating God as a prostitute, expecting Him to give you what you want and then leave you alone until you have another need. Gifts without the giver are absolutely pointless. Allow His blessings to draw you closer into His presence because even though a gift will make you smile, His presence will give you fullness of joy (Ps. 16:11).

He Wants to Know You

If we rely on another believer's life with God, we will always be hindered. We will never actually see and experience God for who He truly is. We will develop ideas about Him that are inconsistent with His character, simply because we never took the time to meet with Him one-on-one. While Jesus was giving His famous Sermon on the Mount, He looked out at a crowd of open ears and hungry hearts and made this statement:

> *Not everyone who says to Me, "Lord, Lord," will enter the kingdom of heaven, but he who does the will of My Father who is in heaven will enter. Many will say to Me on that day, "Lord, Lord, did we not prophesy in Your name, and in Your name cast out demons, and in*

Your name perform many miracles?" And then I will declare to them,
"I never knew you; depart from Me, you who practice lawlessness."

—*Matt. 7:21–23*

These verses are so much more freeing than they have been portrayed. They say that Jesus wants to know you personally. It matters not how many healings you take part in, how many prophetic words you give, or even how many demons you cast out. If you don't actually *know* God on a personal level, then you have missed the very purpose of your existence. You were born for intimacy with Him. Life is not about the list of works you can check off. It is about living your life loving Jesus. When you live your life through love, works will naturally come. These verses take away the pressure to perform and invite us into the joys of truly knowing Him.

No one can love God for you. It is completely up to each individual believer to develop his or her own relationship with God. Jesus paid the price so every person could have equal access to God the Father. There is no longer the need to go through any human on earth to hear from Him or experience His everlasting love. The only thing keeping you from accessing Him today is what you believe about Him. He wants to connect with you every day on a personal level. That is the beauty of the Christian life—that we serve a God who is willing and able to meet with us daily and give us the perfect love that all of us crave.

5

The Journey of Maturity

Life is a journey, a beautiful journey of discovery. Each day we are alive, we are continually experiencing and learning about the world around us. It is hardwired into each of us. The need to discover has helped many skilled men and women invent things that have shaped our culture. Einstein had his theory of relativity, Steve Jobs came up with the iPhone, and Mary Anderson invented windshield wipers. All of them have influenced how we enjoy our brief existence in time. Every day the sun rises, there is a new opportunity to achieve what seemed impossible yesterday.

In the previous chapter, we discussed the starting place of growth in the life of a believer. It was simply an understanding of your personal relationship with God, the idea that truly knowing God is the place from which our entire life begins. In this chapter, let's look at the process of growth. Specifically, let's look at the journey of spiritual maturity, that time between salvation and death. I have wrestled with this idea for some time now and believe I have stumbled on some very freeing revelations that you might also appreciate. As we begin to tackle this, we must first ask this question: What is spiritual maturity?

Maturity Redefined

We would probably all agree that spiritual maturity is a process. Each of us is maturing in Christ every single day of our lives. However, many interpret the maturing believer as one who is becoming more like God. We hear Christians make statements like this: I just want to be more like Jesus today than I was yesterday. However you decide to spin it, the overall message is the same: I'm not like Him yet, but I'm working on it. The implication is that we must work—after we are saved—to become like God. From there, the Christian life becomes a focused attempt to pray enough, read enough, and do enough to somehow transform ourselves into His image and separate ourselves from sin. I agree that we may not be like Him yet in our actions and thoughts, but the Bible is clear that my identity is in His image. In other words, at the core of my being, I am already like Him. Yes, the statement *I want to be all that God wants me to be* is very valid because it expresses the desire to live how God has destined for me to live. However, in order to *be* something in my life, I must first know I *am* something.

Some define Christian maturity as a progressive transformation of our being. They believe that once you say yes to Jesus and make a conscious decision to invite God into your life, you will spend the rest of your life striving to *become* holy and *become* more like God. You may be reading this and agreeing completely with what I just described. However, I have noticed a few inconsistencies with this way of thinking. Although I truly believe that the Holy Spirit is continually working in us, I do not believe He is making us more like Christ. I would like to submit that He is awakening us to the reality of our new Christ-like nature.

The problem I have with the former understanding of maturity is that it focuses on our works. If I must work to be like Him, then He didn't make me in His image. He merely gave me some tools and said *make yourself in My image.* Yet scripture clearly states that our works had nothing to do with our conversion. "For by grace you have been saved through faith; and that not of yourselves, it is the gift of God; not as a result of works, so that no one may boast" (Eph. 2:8–9). Most of us would agree that our works didn't save us. No one is arguing that. So if we believe our works didn't save us, then why would we believe that our works keep us saved? If we believe our works didn't make us holy, why would we believe our works keep us holy, or even make us holier? So why would we believe that our works make us more like Him?

Anytime you incorporate your accomplishments into the gospel message, you completely undermine the cross. The cross was God accomplishing what thousands of years of human attempts never could. This works-centered belief is the very thing the Apostle Paul explicitly called out to the church in Galatia.

> *You foolish Galatians, who has bewitched you, before whose eyes Jesus Christ was publicly portrayed as crucified? This is the only thing I want to find out from you: did you receive the Spirit by the works of the Law, or by hearing with faith? Are you so foolish? Having begun by the Spirit, are you now being perfected by the flesh?*
>
> —Gal. 3:1–3

Paul is drawing their attention to the focus they have placed on their works and the belief that they can perfect themselves in the flesh, or body. He even calls them fools—twice. Although his words are a little more severe than what I would use, he makes a valid point. This idea is still rampant today. Why are we constantly striving to accomplish what Jesus already did for us? Why do we think for a second that we must remold what Jesus re-created?

So what is Christian maturity? Does it come from memorizing the entire Bible? Does it come from praying at least two hours a day? Is the pinnacle of maturity reached by the number of daily good deeds? The truth is, spiritual maturity is not about accumulating external accolades. I define spiritual maturity not as a process of becoming but rather as a journey of discovery. I am not becoming more like God. I am discovering that I am already like God. I am as much like Jesus right now on this earth as I will ever be. No amount of prayer, Bible reading, abstaining from sin, good deeds, fasting, or even church attendance will ever, for one second, make me more in His image than I already am or add any amount of holiness to who I am. This way of looking at it will give you so much freedom that you won't be able to contain yourself.

You Have Already Become Like Him

I will say it again: What you do has nothing to do with your level of holiness. You are already made in His image. You are already like Him—not in one day, not progressively over time as long as you are obedient. You are like Him right now. The starting place for holy living must be this: holiness is who I am. John puts it this way.

> *By this, love is perfected with us, so that we may have confidence in the day of judgment; because as He is, so also are we in this world.*
>
> *—1 John 4:17*

What a beautiful revelation! As He currently is, so we currently are. Rather than spending our lives striving to become more like Jesus, I am invited into an exhilarating journey of discovering my identity and His identity. Therefore, the maturing process of the believer is merely an uncovering of what is already a reality. Once I realize I have been made holy through His blood, it allows me to live a life that is congruent with that holiness. In essence, once I know who I am, I can live accordingly. The desire to sin begins to break away because I am in touch with my re-created reality.

My wife and I have a beautiful son. This kid is the light of our lives. Everything he does is adorable, except maybe his temper tantrums. When he was born, he became my son. That is who he is. Interestingly, he will not spend the rest of his life becoming my son. He is as much my son right now as he will ever be in this life. No amount of obedience to my requests or lack of hissy fits will ever make him more of a son or even a better son. However, he is growing up and maturing. He is learning, but he is not changing who he is; he is discovering who he is. He is discovering how to live as a son, not becoming a son. So it is with us as Christians. We are not becoming sons and daughters of God; we have already become his children. We are not becoming more like Him; we are already like Him. Maturity is an invitation to discover who you are, not a process of becoming who He wants you to be. Holiness is manifested on the outside once it is realized on the inside. Our maturing process is learning to live as the holy person He has recreated, living with integrity, aligning our words with our deeds.

The Bible is very clear that we have been set apart and made holy. What an important thing to realize as a Christian! If we start from *I am holy* rather than *I need to be holy*, we are free to live according to our new nature rather than strive to change our nature. That, in turn, allows us to live *from* holiness rather than *for* holiness. Here are a few verses that explain this truth. The word *sanctified* in these verses means *to make holy.*

> *By this will we **have been** sanctified through the offering of the body of Jesus Christ once for all (emphasis added).*
>
> *—Heb. 10:10*

> *For by one offering He has perfected for all time those who **are** sanctified (emphasis added).*
>
> *—Heb. 10:14*

*But you were washed, but you **were** sanctified, but you were justified in the name of the Lord Jesus Christ and in the Spirit of our God (emphasis added).*

—1 Cor. 6:11

*To the church of God which is at Corinth, to those who **have been** sanctified in Christ Jesus, saints by calling, with all who in every place call on the name of our Lord Jesus Christ, their Lord and ours (emphasis added).*

—1 Cor. 1:2

*To open their eyes so that they may turn from darkness to light and from the dominion of Satan to God, that they may receive forgiveness of sins and an inheritance among those who **have been** sanctified by faith in Me (emphasis added).*

—Acts 26:18

Underneath it all, we are truly holy and spotless—sanctified. God didn't cover our sinfulness up with a towel, merely giving us the appearance of holiness and masking who we really are. He killed us and then re-created us into a perfectly pure person (Romans 6:6).

The Mirror

I have been known to frequently look at myself in a mirror. My wife likes to joke about how I spend more time in front of a mirror than she does. She's right. I'll admit that I probably spend an unhealthy amount of time gazing at myself. But I want to make sure I look presentable, and the purpose of a mirror, after all, is to allow you to see yourself. James speaks of a mirror in James 1:23–24:

For if anyone is a hearer of the word and not a doer, he is like a man who looks at his natural face in a mirror; for once he has looked at himself and gone away, he has immediately forgotten what kind of person he was.

The typical message preached regarding these verses is that we need to strive to do what the word says and that we are commissioned to work harder to do what God commands. Even though we should obviously do what the word says, I believe there is also an important solution hidden in these verses that will allow us to live as doers.

James is making the distinction that if someone isn't doing what God has said, that person is like one who has walked away from a mirror and forgotten what he or she looked like. At first glance this may seem confusing. What mirror is he referring to? That becomes clear in the following verse:

But one who looks intently at the perfect law, the law of liberty, and abides by it, not having become a forgetful hearer but an effectual doer, this man will be blessed in what he does.

—James 1:25

Here we see that the perfect law is the mirror. Now we must ask, *What is the perfect law?* We could accurately conclude that he isn't referring to the old covenant due to Paul's words in the book of Romans about being dead to the law. I would like to submit that the perfect law is referring to Jesus. He has fulfilled the law. He is the image of the invisible God. He is the mirror we look at and see who we are. We are now the image of Jesus. Many believe we are the mirrors that reflect Him. However, James concludes that He is the mirror. What is the difference? If He is the mirror, then I am not reflecting Him—I am seeing who I am *in* who He is.

I am Christ-like in my truest identity. In order to do what God's word says, I must realize and remember who I am by staring into the eyes of Jesus, into the mirror and the perfect law of liberty. If I stay focused on Him, I will live like He intends. When I see what He looks like, I see who I have become. Am I God? No! But I have been created in His image and in His likeness.

Paul uses the same mirror analogy in his second letter to the church at Corinth.

But we all, with unveiled face, beholding as in a mirror the glory of the Lord, are being transformed into the same image from glory to glory, just as from the Lord, the Spirit.

—*2 Cor. 3:18*

There is so much going on in this verse, so much that it could be the focus of my next book. But for the time being, I will keep it simple. *Unveiled* is a reference to a Christian's new reality. When we said yes to God, the veil that kept us from clearly seeing Him was removed.

After the veil is removed and we clearly see God, we realize that He is the mirror in which we are able to see ourselves. If at any moment I do anything that is incongruent with His nature, it is not because I am less holy. It is because I have forgotten who I truly am. My new nature is displayed in Him. When I see Him, I see who I have become. I am already made in His image.

It is believed that the mirrors used in Paul's time were not as good as the ones we have today. The mirrors were made from highly polished metals instead of glass. That allowed somewhat of a reflection, but it was a limited one. Knowing this, Paul's words in 1 Corinthians 13 make more sense.

For now we see in a mirror dimly, but then face to face; now I know in part, but then I will know fully just as I also have been fully known.

—*1 Cor. 13:12*

We see ourselves dimly until we see Jesus face-to-face. Only when He returns to take us home will we be fully enlightened to who we have been during our entire Christian walk. Why? Because only then will we see him face-to-face in His perfection. Then we will know fully just as we have been fully known.

> *Beloved, now we are children of God, and it has not appeared as yet what we will be. We know that when He appears, we will be like Him, because we will see Him just as He is.*
>
> —*1 John 3:2*

I must understand that my identity is in His image. I am not striving to become like Him. I am discovering, by staring into the mirror, who He has made me to be. Once I truly know who I am, I will inevitably model God's holiness to the world around me. Everything flows from identity. If I want to walk like Christ, I must first know I am made to look like Christ. Christian maturity is a process led by the Holy Spirit that allows me to continually uncover my true image. Don't allow the enemy to plant lies that cause you to forget who you are.

Stop Pretending

I remember a time recently when I decided to voice some of my concerns to God. I am not the type of person who likes to beat around the bush with God. I figure that since God already knows what I'm thinking, I might as well willingly tell Him how I feel. In this particular moment, I was upset about a reoccurring struggle I had been dealing with for as long as I could remember.

I shouted, "God I know that you have saved me and made me new, so why do I continually fall back into the same sin over and over again?" I was hoping to hear Him apologize. Part of me wanted to blame God. But deep down, I knew it was something on my end. I knew there was a lie somewhere in my mind that I had acquired from an unknown source, so I was relentless in my search. As I demanded an answer for my desperate question, I clearly heard His voice inside say this: *Because you're pretending.* Once I was through battling with whether or not that was Him, I became even angrier. It made absolutely no sense to me. *I'm pretending?* I heard it again: *You're pretending.*

As I continued to hash out my feelings with the Lord, He repeatedly said the same words I had now grown to despise: *Because you're pretending.* Finally, after my vacillating input had reached its peak, He shouted, *Stop Pretending!* So there I sat in complete silence, contemplating His last statement.

Time went by as I wrestled for an explanation. Suddenly I was prompted to look up the definition of *pretend.* So I searched on Google for a definition. Here is what came up: "speak and act so as to make it appear that something is the case when in fact it is not." Although I was aware of what *pretend* meant, something came alive inside that filled me with extreme encouragement as I read the brief definition online. At that point, I had absolutely no language to explain what I was feeling. All I knew was that God was giving me hope.

As the moments progressed, the Lord showed me a mental motion picture that I will never forget. In this visual, I was invited to a party. I received my invitation through the mail and was excited about attending. Although I didn't recognize who was hosting the party or where it was located, the address on the invitation seemed to demand my presence. I followed the directions and arrived at the gorgeous house. Once I rang the doorbell, the host answered the door with a smile. It was in that moment that I realized I was attending a costume party. "I don't have a costume," I said, wondering what would happen next. With joy in his eyes, the host said, "That's all right, we provide the costumes."

I eagerly entered the door and received my costume. In this picture the Lord gave me, the costume I was wearing was vague and irrelevant. All I could gather from this was that I was wearing someone else's costume. So I walked around, talking and meeting people while portraying the characteristics of the costume I was wearing. All of a sudden, I realized who was hosting the party. It was Satan. I was at Satan's party wearing one of Satan's costumes. Then I heard the Lord's soft voice again: *Stop pretending.* I sat in shock as I realized what God was saying to me: *The reason you are still struggling with this is because you believe it is who you are and have unknowingly acquired the desires of someone else. That's not who you are; it's only who you think you are. Take off the costume and stop pretending.* I had walked away from the mirror of Jesus and completely forgotten what I looked like.

So many of us make wrong decisions, fall into temptation, and let life tear us down simply because we have forgotten who we are. We are wearing someone else's costume. This is a call to remembrance, a journey of discovery. How beautiful is each moment when I can unearth the reality of my sanctification in Christ. How wonderful is the moment I discover my true identity. When you discover who you are, you realize who you aren't. When you realize who you aren't, you can put it off and live free.

The Journey of Maturity

I have been invited into a lifelong journey of a God-led discovery of what He has already made perfect. I am a tree planted in God that will not wither. I have no reason to fear when negative circumstances arise. I have been perfected through Christ's finished work on the cross and have strength in every moment (Heb. 10:10). I was born to thrive. The only thing that keeps me from living this truth is my knowledge of who I am in Christ. Paul gives us great insight into our process of maturity:

> *Therefore we do not lose heart, but though our outer man is decaying, yet our inner man is being renewed day by day.*

> —*2 Cor. 4:16*

With the wrong eyes, we could see this as a supporting statement for progressively becoming holier in our spirit. This can't be true because we know that Jesus has already perfected us. So what is Paul saying? The word *renewed* is used exclusively by Paul and appears only twice in the New Testament. According to *Thayer's Greek-English Lexicon of the New Testament*, this word means "to cause to grow up."[1] Paul is speaking about our maturing process. Although our physical body is decaying, our spirit is maturing every day. We are continually growing in Christ and learning to manifest the holiness He has already instilled in us.

The second time this word is used is in Colossians. Here we have a better context for understanding this specific word.

> *Do not lie to one another, since you laid aside the old self with its evil practices, and have put on the new self who is being renewed to a true knowledge according to the image of the One who created him.*

> —*Col. 3:9–10*

We can clearly see that the renewing process is growing in the true understanding of the image of Christ. We are not becoming like Christ, we are renewing our mind to see Jesus in His perfection, ultimately seeing ourselves correctly. A couple of verses down, we are called "those who have been chosen of God, holy and beloved" (Col. 3:12). Because of this, we can wake up every morning holy in Christ, ready to live like Him.

If you back up to verses 5–9, you will see that Paul lists a bunch of dos and don'ts. Rather than looking at them as a daunting list to measure up to, they are a beautiful revelation of our ability to live a holy life. Paul says in verse 9 that we *can* put off the actions of sin because we have already put off the old self: "since you *laid* [past tense] aside the old self with its evil practices" (emphasis added). We can put away all evil deeds because we have already put off our evil self. Paul says it like this in Romans:

> *Knowing this, that our old self was crucified with Him, in order that our body of sin might be done away with, so that we would no longer be slaves to sin; for he who has died is freed from sin.*
>
> —*Rom. 6:6*

Your old self has been killed off, and a new self has been created, one after the likeness of the creator. Don't be like I was and continue to wear the old costume, walking and talking as someone else. Cast that thing off, because it is not an accurate representation of who you really are.

As Close As We Can Possibly Be in This Life

There is a common misconception that says we must strive to be closer to God. One can even argue that maturity is an attempt to gain more of God. Even though I believed that for a long time, I recently began to question this idea after reading a certain verse. We have already touched on part of this passage earlier in this chapter, but I would like to look at it again along with its preceding verses.

> *Whoever confesses that Jesus is the Son of God, God abides in him, and he in God. We have come to know and have believed the love which God has for us. God is love, and the one who abides in love abides in God, and God abides in him. By this, love is perfected with us, so that we may have confidence in the day of judgment; because as He is, so also are we in this world.*
>
> —*1 John 4:15–17*

If God truly abides in us, how is it possible to gain more of Him? If we have been filled with His spirit, why would we believe we must get closer to Him? We are as close to God as we can possibly be in this life. I realize that once our earthly bodies die, we will receive glorified bodies that will physically dwell with God in heaven for all eternity (Phil. 3:12). But on this side of physical death, we are as close to God as we can possibly be. Yes, in a sense, it is a mental closeness that progresses with maturity. We are continually discovering how much of God we already have and the true power of our union with Christ. But the fact that I am in God and that God is in me is true no matter what I choose to believe as a Christian.

There is no place I can go that God isn't there with me. David understood this when he wrote, "If I ascend to heaven, You are there; If I make my bed in Sheol, behold, You are there" (Ps. 139:8). For Christians, God is inescapable. No matter where we go and no matter what we do, He is right there with us, around us, and in us.

Even sin can't separate us from God any longer. The sins that Christians choose to commit have no effect on hindering the indwelling of God's spirit within them. Many want to believe that sin still separates the Christian from God, but the truth is that Jesus died so sin would have no power.

He made Him who knew no sin to be sin on our behalf, so that we might become the righteousness of God in Him.

—*2 Cor. 5:21*

Wow! Jesus became sin! That means when Jesus died, He died as sin. However, when He rose again, sin stayed dead. Jesus was glorified, but sin was buried. By dying as sin, he completely removed the power of sin from the earth. The only power sin has today is an illusion. Does that mean we should sin? Absolutely not! You are considered holy; therefore, you *can* and *must* live holy.

Because we are in Christ, we have been set free from sin. We are able to live completely holy lives as Christians because we have been re-created into His image and continue to hold His very presence within our being. When you understand the reality of Christ in you, the hope of glory (Col. 1:27), you will walk as a confident child of God with full assurance that He will never leave you or forsake you.

Our Responsibility

As we reach the end of this chapter, I hope you aren't misunderstanding my premise. I am in no way reducing our personal involvement in this life. We still have an important responsibility as Christians to make a conscious decision to follow Christ. Just because Christ did it all for us doesn't mean we should do whatever we want in this life, good or bad. There is still a standard of holy living that God has for those who love Him. I am responsible for my own actions and decisions. However, if I am burdened with the belief that I am becoming holy through my actions, an excuse to create exceptions for sin can bubble up in my thinking. I could say I'm not there yet and knowingly walk in the same patterns of sin I did as a non-Christian. I could also become discouraged due to my distorted belief that I must try harder to become holy. My responsibility of holy living ceases to be a burden when I discover that I am like Him. From that place, I can be my true self. It is not some vague misinterpretation of a whimsical feeling, but rather the undeniable being that He has re-created through His sacrifice.

God commands us to be holy as He is holy. That is impossible if we believe we have to progressively make ourselves holier. I am one who believes that God does not set us up to fail with His commands. If He has commanded something, it is only because it is possible.

As obedient children, do not be conformed to the former lusts which were yours in your ignorance, but like the Holy One who called you, be holy yourselves also in all your behavior; because it is written, "YOU SHALL BE HOLY, FOR I AM HOLY."

—1 Pet. 1:14–16

Notice how Peter is comparing the command to be holy with behavior. It isn't an invitation to make yourself holy like God. He is explaining that He has made you as holy as He is. So live like it. When I realize that the starting place—rather than the finish line—is holiness, I stop striving to change who I am and return to the mirror to see what is real. As I stare intently into the eyes of God, I am able to mimic His every move. The walk then becomes effortless because I clearly see the one I was created to look like.

Temptations will come, but when you know who you are, what is a temptation? Jesus never gave in to the enemy's temptations in the wilderness because it wasn't appealing to Him. He knew who He was, and no one could convince Him otherwise. The bread that Satan attempted to give Jesus was nothing compared to the bread God the Father was already giving. God has already prepared you a table in the presence of your enemies (Ps. 23:5). When you recognize the table in front of you, filled with holy food, the bread of temptation loses its appeal.

We are able to see a transformation into holy behavior when we see ourselves as He does: holy. If you are struggling to live up to the standard of grace, it isn't because Jesus didn't do a good enough job of making you new. It is only because you have yet to discover the perfection He has already given you.

The Holy Spirit is constantly working within us to empower us to live as those who are already made in His image. Continue to allow Him to lead you and guide you into all truth as you travel on this journey of spiritual maturity that leads to a lifestyle of holiness.

6

Connected Conversation

It amazes me how far communication has come in our society. We have amazing capabilities today that the generations before us couldn't even dream of. Our ability to communicate with one another has greatly evolved over the centuries. Hundreds of years ago, delivering an important message was a very tiring task that involved a handwritten letter and a risky journey. Nowadays, having a conversation with someone in another country is as simple as dialing a number on my smartphone or sending an email from my laptop. I even have the ability to voice my opinions to the entire world through social media websites with the click of a button or the tap of a finger. But despite the many ways of communicating in our world today, nothing can replace face-to-face conversation. It is a vital part of humanity.

Prayer in its simplest form is communication with God. It is an earthly form of face-to-face communication with Him that is absolutely necessary in the life of a believer. Those who go without prayer constantly find themselves in what feels like a dry season with nothing left to give to others. There is a very unique verse in Exodus 33:11 about Moses and his relationship with God: "Thus the LORD used to speak to Moses face to face, just as a man speaks to his friend." If this level of intimate conversation could exist between God and a member of the old covenant, how much more could a son

75

or daughter under a new covenant experience. Our spiritual success is dependent on our ability to speak to and hear from God the Father in heaven. But it's hard to hear from God when we don't listen. Our ability to communicate with God face-to-face is vital to staying well-watered, and there are no alternatives. Jesus died so we would have an unhindered connection with Him, a place where we can engage in conversation with God Himself.

The Jesus Way to Pray

If there was ever a person who could show us the perfect way to pray, it would be Jesus Christ. He was the master of communicating with God the Father, and out of that intimacy came His well-known life and ministry that we read about. In Matthew 6, Jesus gives us insight into the beauty of prayer. The first thing He tells us is how *not* to pray.

> *When you pray, you are not to be like the hypocrites; for they love to stand and pray in the synagogues and on the street corners so that they may be seen by men. Truly I say to you, they have their reward in full. And when you are praying, do not use meaningless repetition as the Gentiles do, for they suppose that they will be heard for their many words. So do not be like them; for your Father knows what you need before you ask Him.*
>
> *—Matt. 6:5,7–8*

We have all heard the prayers of the attention seekers, the ones who throw out huge words and wail out their requests. Sometimes these prayers are genuine and necessary, but other times they are just wasted words. Jesus tells us in this passage that God is not concerned with poetic phrases and loud tones. He doesn't want a religious activity; He wants a genuine conversation.

I feel it is important to quickly distinguish between two types of prayer. One is an individual's personal prayer life, and the other is the corporate prayer of a group of believers. The personal prayer is when you meet with God one-on-one to build intimacy. The corporate prayer is when a collection of believers come together in unity with one mind and one purpose. Each type has its benefits. Jesus is in no way diminishing corporate prayer in these verses but is talking more about the personal prayer life that we all can have with God the Father. In either setting, it is important to realize that your heart is more important than your language. I spent many years thinking my prayers weren't good enough and was embarrassed by any chance I was given to pray. It took me a long time to realize that 10 words from a pure heart are better than hundreds of words from a religious poet. But there is nothing wrong with wanting to expand your prayer vocabulary. Prayer creates intimacy, and out of intimacy comes new language to communicate. Continue in daily conversation and watch your dialect transform.

The main goal is to be heard by God, not people. If human approval is all you seek when you lift up your problems or your praises, then that is the only reward you will receive. And if you ask me, it's like getting socks for Christmas.

The next point Jesus makes on prayer is *where* to pray.

> *But you, when you pray, go into your inner room, close your door and pray to your Father who is in secret, and your Father who sees what is done in secret will reward you.*
>
> —*Matt. 6:6*

Here Jesus gives us a perfect place to seek the Lord. It is commonly known among Christians as "the secret place"—a place where it is just you and God. I once thought when Jesus said "close your door" He was speaking literally, but now I see this verse in a different light. I believe He is telling us to shut out all the competing voices around us and listen closely to His voice. It is easy to get preoccupied with the busy-ness of our lives. Our job, our family, and our hobbies sometimes compete with God for our time, but Jesus is telling us to get away from (close the door on) anything that could pull our attention from Him in that moment. The secret place doesn't have to be a specific room with walls and a door; it is a state of mind that we enter into where we can focus on Him without distractions. That being said, sometimes it is best to have a physical room that is just for you and the Lord, a place where you are free to be vulnerable and intimate.

Next, Jesus gives us His layout for prayer. There have been many sermons preached and books written that have done a great job explaining the Lord's Prayer. I am not going to look in depth at these verses. I will just give you a quick overview of what I have come to understand. Before we dive into this prayer, I want to stress that this is not a formula. The idea is not to go to God the Father with a transcript. Jesus merely outlines key points that are common in prayer. How you converse with God is 100 percent your business and your preference. If we attempt to mimic someone else's spiritual life, we lose authenticity and step into religious formulas that actually accomplish the opposite of God's will for us. As we go through each verse, keep in mind that each principle of prayer will look different in the context of *your* life. My purpose in the following breakdown is only to bring a better understanding to prayer. Let's take a look at the first verse.

Pray, then, in this way:
"Our Father who is in heaven,
Hallowed be Your name."

—*Matt. 6:9*

I always heard the word *hallowed* growing up, but I never knew what it meant. I read it, remembered it, and recited it, but I never understood it. The Greek word for *hallowed* is *hagiazō*, which means to make holy or sanctify. Basically, what we are saying as we pray is this: May your name be kept holy. This is the language of a worshiper. The Jesus-modeled prayer begins and ends with worship.

I have heard Bill Johnson, senior pastor of Bethel Church in Redding, California, say that if he has 10 minutes to pray, he will spend eight minutes worshiping. This is a beautiful way to begin your time with the Lord. As we begin to lift up His name and declare who He is, it changes the way we see what we came to pray about. The best prayers are those that begin with worship because rather than unload all our junk, we minister to Him while reminding ourselves of who He is and what He has done. It is important that we as Christians consciously consider this. Our heart begins to focus on the true nature of God, allowing our voice to express our true love for Him. We move from using robotic repetition to romantic language. Let's look at the next verse.

> *Your kingdom come.*
> *Your will be done,*
> *On earth as it is in heaven.*

> *—Matt. 6:10*

Here, Jesus is giving us permission to pray out God's will and heaven's reality over every situation. In doing so, we remove from earth the things that don't exist in heaven. It is one of the best examples of God's will: heaven on earth. We are asking God to bring the realities of heaven to the world we live in, that His world would invade our world, that whatever is true there will be true here. Obviously, heaven will not come in its fullness until the triumphant return of our king, but until that day, we can continually pull from heaven the things needed for a supernatural, thriving lifestyle here on earth.

It is His desire to see us use the things we have been given access to in heaven here on earth. If I am rooted in the rivers of heaven, then I am excused from living a natural life. I am a supernatural being, rooted in supernatural waters with access to supernatural resources. Matthew 6:10 assures us that we can thrive in this world no matter the situation.

We need to understand that this idea of heaven on earth is not solely for us. If we can bring heaven to earth, then not only are we positively affected, but everything and everyone we encounter are also positively affected. The best way to bring lost souls into the kingdom of heaven is to accurately display what heaven looks like. We are not confined to only speak words about a greater reality, but we can actually bring that reality here to this earth.

Give us this day our daily bread.

—Matt. 6:11

Here, we are asking the Lord not for sandwich ingredients, but for the things needed for everyday living. Whatever our needs may be, whether they are clothes, food, or finances, we can boldly ask Him, fully expecting Him to deliver (1 John 5:14). He has heaven's eternal resources and is able and willing to distribute them to those who ask Him without doubting. If we can grasp that simple concept, it will change how we see what we have and what we are capable of receiving.

I would also like to submit that God not only gives us what we need but also what we want. Whenever my parents bought me a gift for Christmas, they never gave me what I needed; they always gave me what I *wanted*. In Matthew 7:11, Jesus says, "If you then, being evil, know how to give good gifts to your children, how much more will your Father who is in heaven give what is good to those who ask Him!" I am not saying that He will always give us exactly what we want, exactly when we want it. He is not looking to produce entitled children who have no need for faith and patience. I am simply saying that God cares about the little things. What is important to you is important to Him.

And forgive us our debts, as we also have forgiven our debtors.

—*Matt. 6:12*

In the first half of this verse, He is telling us to allow the Lord to forgive our sins. When Jesus died on the cross, it allowed God to forgive all sin in the world, including the sins that were yet to be committed (Rom. 6:10). Trust is established when we are willing to give God the sins we have committed. That shows true repentance. Repentance isn't just changing the way we act; it is changing the way we think. Only when we truly change the way we think can we change the way we live. Our behaviors come from our beliefs. When we allow God to forgive us, it shows that we acknowledge our shortcomings, that we trust Him, and that we are ready to let Him renew our minds. It releases any guilt or shame that the enemy has attached and allows us to move forward with hope.

The second half of this verse speaks to unforgiveness. Those who allow unforgiveness to exist within them begin to produce bitterness, hate, and other unhealthy attitudes. Unforgiveness will absolutely destroy a healthy perspective and send us spiraling down an endless dark hole. Anne Lamott wrote in her book *Traveling Mercies: Some Thoughts on Faith*, "Not forgiving is like drinking rat poison and then waiting for the rat to die."[1]

The only person that unforgiveness destroys is you. Go to God and allow Him to change your heart and mind about those who have hurt you. The best thing to do when a person hurts you is to pray for them directly (Luke 6:28). Pray for their health, prosperity, family—whatever you would want someone to pray for you. Of course, that is easier said than done. The last thing you want to do for someone who has severely wronged you is to pronounce blessings over them. But as you begin to speak blessings over them, it will change the way you see them. And how you see someone determines how you treat them.

And do not lead us into temptation, but deliver us from evil. For Yours is the kingdom and the power and the glory forever. Amen.

—Matt. 6:13

Here is the opportunity to receive the strength necessary to make it through any situation. Jesus told his disciples to "pray that you may not enter into temptation" (Luke 22:46). When we have done all we know to do, we can rest in Him and find our strength. He gives us the ability to withstand any and all temptations the enemy approaches us with. The last part of this verse includes more worship. I believe the best prayers start and end with worship. The worst case scenario is that God gets His rightful praise and you leave encouraged.

When Jesus gave this model for prayer, His intentions were not to create another religious declaration but to provide an outline of how to go to God the Father. This prayer is an example, but it is not the end all. It includes topical elements that get us started with our prayers. The beauty of prayer is that we can express *our* heart in *our* language to *our* heavenly father.

He Heard You

Some of us have believed a lie that says God doesn't listen when we pray. I have believed that, too, in different stages of my life. Often, we believe we are unworthy or incapable of talking to God, but nothing could be further from the truth. Although it sometimes seems hard for us to hear His voice, it is not hard for Him to hear ours.

This is the confidence which we have before Him, that, if we ask anything according to His will, He hears us. And if we know that He hears us in whatever we ask, we know that we have the requests which we have asked from Him.

—*1 John 5:14–15*

God has no problem hearing the voices of His sons and daughters. When we pray to God, we can have complete assurance that He is listening and that He is willing to give us the answers we need. Believers' prayers are powerful, and nothing can stop them from reaching God. The enemy knows this and is persistent in filling our minds with lies. He persuades us to believe that our prayers are too small or too large. Because of the power and importance prayer plays in believers' lives, Satan will do anything he can to keep us from talking to God. Don't buy it. Your secret place isn't stifled by the enemy's screams.

Wait for It

There are times in our lives when we don't receive answers to our prayers right away. When that happens, it is easy to become discouraged and believe that God either wasn't listening or doesn't care. But I have found one thing to be true. Just because there is no instant answer doesn't mean He has ignored our request.

I like things to be instant—instant food, instant movie streaming, instant workout results. I am not big on waiting. If you look at our culture today, you will find this mindset running rampant. The world we live in caters to the impatient. We have fast-food restaurants, drive-through banks, and self-checkout machines. The minute we see lines or have to wait for something, we begin to sweat on the inside. But walking with God requires patience.

Galatians 5:22–23 includes patience in the fruit of the spirit. Romans 8:25 says we wait patiently for what we can't see. Apparently, patience is a big deal to God. Just because the answer isn't instant doesn't mean the prayer has been ignored. We must believe that He heard what we said and will give us what we asked according to His will. Using patience is vital to thriving in life. Without patience, we live as the type of people who can't enjoy anything because we are so caught up in complaining about the wait. But the wait is part of the journey. If we want to enjoy the journey, we must accept the wait. If we stay persistent in what we are praying for and do not doubt, we are qualified to receive. Our ability to wait determines our capability to receive.

A Man with a Withered Hand

Prayer is essential in the life of a Christian. It involves stretching out our hearts and minds to God while building a relational connection that cannot be broken. There is a unique story in three of the four Gospels that beautifully represents prayer. In this story, Jesus encounters a man who is in desperate need of His healing touch. The story goes like this.

> On another Sabbath He entered the synagogue and was teaching; and there was a man there whose right hand was withered. The scribes and the Pharisees were watching Him closely to see if He healed on the Sabbath, so that they might find reason to accuse Him. But He knew what they were thinking, and He said to the man with the withered hand, "Get up and come forward!" And he got up and came forward. And Jesus said to them, "I ask you, is it lawful to do good or to do harm on the Sabbath, to save a life or to destroy it?" After looking around at them all, He said to him, "Stretch out your hand!" And he did so; and his hand was restored. But they themselves were filled with rage, and discussed together what they might do to Jesus.
>
> —Luke 6:6–11

These verses tell us that the man Jesus met had a withered hand. The word *withered* is defined in this context in *Thayer's Greek-English Lexicon* as "of members of the body deprived of their natural juices, shrunk, wasted, withered."[2] The man's hand literally did not have the proper bodily fluids flowing through it to keep it healthy and whole. This man had a problem. His hand had been deprived of its necessary liquids and was in desperate need of revival.

Jesus saw this and told him to come near. It is interesting that the Bible doesn't say the man asked to be healed. It seems he was just in the right place at the right time. Jesus then turned to the man and said, "Stretch out your hand." In several places in the Gospels, we see that Jesus stretched out His own hand (Mark 1:41, Matt. 14:31), but here, Jesus tells the man to stretch out his hand.

In Luke's account of this story, he adds a detail that Matthew and Mark chose to leave out. He specifies which hand it was: the right hand. *Right hand* is a phrase peppered throughout the Bible that usually represents a place of honor or authority. For instance, Jesus is seated at the right hand of God (Rom. 8:34), His rightful place of authority. The specificity of *right hand* tells me that his ailment might be a little deeper than just an inconvenience. His very symbol of authority had been drained.

Sometimes in our lives, we encounter situations that seem to steal from us the very authority that Jesus has given us. We feel drained. Trials come, and we find ourselves withered, desperately needing the Lord to revive us. But in those moments, we cannot let the fact of the trial change the truth of our nature. Jesus delegated His authority to all believers (Luke 10:19). Even when life tries to shrivel what Jesus paid for, we can confidently proclaim the authority that we have been given. Nothing can take our authority from us unless we willingly let go of it.

Jesus could have laid hands on this man and healed him, but instead, He looks for an obedient act. God can give you what you need at any time during your day, but He wants you to stretch out, in prayer, those areas that seem to be lacking in your life. He wants you to stretch out to Him what needs watering. God does not want to retrieve our prayers; He wants to receive them.

My mother is a junior high school teacher, and I was "privileged" as a kid to attend the same school where she worked. When your mother teaches at your school, there is absolutely nothing you can get away with. She seemed to know what I did before I ever did it. But at the end of each day, she would still ask me how my day was and what I did. Why? Because she didn't know? That's highly unlikely. When I willingly gave her information about my day, whether or not she already knew, it showed that I trusted her, and that built a stronger relational connection between us.

Many people are unwilling to approach God with issues because they believe He already knows what is going on. Although it is true that He knows, He still wants you to come to Him with anything and everything. It shows that you trust Him with your life. Don't expect God to just intervene if you are unwilling to tell Him what is going on in your world. He will not take from you what you are unwilling to give. That would be considered stealing, and the last time I checked, that was the thief's territory (John 10:10).

It was after the man stretched out his hand that he received his healing. What do you think would have happened if he had kept it to himself? He probably would have held on to his problem for the rest of his life. It takes humility to go to the Lord with areas that have been infected by the enemy. But if we humble ourselves before the Lord and lift up our problems to Him, He will always lift us up (James 4:10).

After this humbling act, the Bible says his hand was restored. That word *restored* means to return to its former state. Jesus didn't just patch up his problem; He completely restored it to a former state where the ailment didn't exist. Too often we run to other sources, expecting them to bring about complete restoration, but instead, they become Band-Aid remedies that temporarily cover up our wounds rather than remove them.

Whenever we encounter tough situations, it is imperative that we lift them up to Him in prayer so He can lift us up in His strength. When living water touches what is withered in our lives, it gives us the nourishment and the encouragement necessary to continue this journey. As we communicate with God through the act of prayer, we regain the strength we need.

Lacking Nothing

Without constant conversation with God, we begin to allow the enemy's voice to come in and speak lies. We then allow those lies to take root in our minds, causing us to partner with his words of death. That's the enemy's biggest tactic, to convince you that you lack something. However, in Christ, we no longer lack anything.

> *Grace and peace be multiplied to you in the knowledge of God and of Jesus our Lord; seeing that His divine power has granted to us everything pertaining to life and godliness, through the true knowledge of Him who called us by His own glory and excellence.*
>
> *—2 Pet. 1:2–3*

Look at part of that verse again. It says He has "granted us everything pertaining to life and godliness." Because of Jesus, we lack nothing. The issue is that when we stop communicating with God, we are subject to the enemy's lies. We forget who we are and who He is. Yet if the Lord and I stay in constant communication, He enforces the truth of our relationship, and I am invited to discover more of what our relationship offers. I am continually growing in the knowledge of Him and unraveling everything that is available in Him.

We are already connected to God through salvation. The cross gave us that. This is made plain in John 15 where Jesus speaks of the branches (us) abiding in the vine (Jesus). Prayer is not what holds that connection. We don't pray *for* connection, we pray *from* connection. When that mental shift takes place, our prayers move from desperate pleas to connected conversation. We know we are not striving to get something from Him but abiding in perfect unity. We aren't commanded to pray; we are invited to.

Prayer isn't just confined to asking God for things. He is not a genie. If we return to the model of the Lord's Prayer at the beginning of this chapter, we will find that prayer includes much more. It's all about communication. Without a healthy prayer life, we will not be able to thrive in all seasons like Jeremiah 17 states. Even though we are rooted in heaven and have access to a limitless world, avoiding communication with the one who gave us all things would contradict God's ultimate purpose. We have been placed in His world to be with Him. God still speaks to us today, and we as believers have been given ears that are fully capable of hearing His voice.

7

Our Daily Diet

Every now and then when I eat at a restaurant, I am unable to finish my meal, and I ask for a to-go box. That allows me to take what is left over to my house, put it in the refrigerator, and eat it later in the week (that is, if I remember to grab it off the table before I leave). When the time comes that I find myself hungry again, I pull it out, pop it in the microwave, and finish it. But no matter what type of food it was, it never tastes as good as it did when it was fresh. No matter how much I paid for it and no matter how tasty it was, it never holds its flavor overnight.

The same is often true for our conversations with God. Sometimes, we just want to reheat and eat what God gave us yesterday. But the truth is, God has new things for us every day. Sometimes, we believe that one conversation with Him will suffice for several weeks or even several months. But conversing with Him daily is absolutely crucial if we wish to live a well-watered life. He wants to be part of our lives, not just our pasts. I can't expect to maintain a healthy, thriving lifestyle if I have not made Him the priority of my life. His being present everyday gives me the strength to go forward in this world. I was built for continuous intimacy with Him.

Today Is a New Day

After the Israelites walked though the Red Sea and escaped the pursuing Egyptians, they entered into the wilderness. It was during this time that hunger struck, and they collectively began to complain to Moses. But God had compassion and rained down quail for meat and manna for bread. However, there were certain guidelines that came with this miracle bread from above. The Israelites were told to only gather what they could eat in one day and by no means were they to save any for the following day unless the following day happened to be a Sabbath. It was commanded that the Sabbath be kept holy and free from labor. But as it turns out, some of them didn't listen. Imagine that! I'm sure none of us can relate. They gathered as much as possible, expecting to have an abundance that would last for days. But the Bible tells us this:

> *But they did not listen to Moses, and some left part of it until morning, and it bred worms and became foul; and Moses was angry with them.*
>
> —*Exod. 16:20*

The food saved from the previous day became rotten and could not be consumed. This gives us insight into our lives with God. Too often, many of us rely on an encounter we had with Him yesterday to give us the encouragement needed for today. But God has a different diet plan for us. If we rely on yesterday's supply, our lives eventually begin to dry up. I can't expect my life to have a healthy appearance if I am living on last week's conversation with God. That isn't to say that what God has given us in the past is unimportant. There have been many words God has spoken to me about my future that have not come to pass, and I continually replay them and receive life from them. But to neglect Him today because yesterday was so good is the opposite of what the Lord wants. His will is that each encounter with Him draws us closer to Him. Just because God is a God of abundance doesn't mean that I get to coast on previous times with Him. God actually could be saying the exact same thing He spoke yesterday, but it is important for me to know that He is repeating Himself and that I am not just blindly following a past voice. He wants to meet with me daily. My ability to thrive today is contingent upon my ability to receive His daily bread.

My wife loves it when I spend time with her. Whether it is binge watching TV shows or taking a stroll through the park, she values every second we spend together. Afterwards she is extremely satisfied, and as author and pastor Gary Chapman would say, her "love tank" is full. But an important thing I have realized in our relationship is that these times don't roll over to the next day. It may be an amazing memory, but she still expects me to spend time with her and show her affection every day. No matter how good one day was for her, it is never good enough for the next day.

Let's say that my wife and I had a perfect evening together. We went on a date that consisted of dinner, a movie, and a walk that included wonderful, intimate conversation. We could physically feel the love radiating between us. When we returned home, she was able to go to sleep that night knowing that she was deeply loved by her spouse. But what if I woke up the next day and didn't say one word to her. Eventually she would wonder why things changed all of a sudden. She would want to know why I was avoiding her. I would say, "Because I talked to you yesterday." She would certainly be left questioning my love for her. And I guarantee she would not be happy.

God is the same. His passion is to be with His children. He doesn't want us to avoid Him today just because we had a conversation with Him yesterday. Genesis tells us that God once walked with Adam and Eve in the cool of the day. Sadly, the two of them eventually separated themselves from God due to the decisions they made. They believed a lie and chose death rather than life. But God was not content to see His beloved only from a distance. So He spent the entire Old Testament revealing His love and uncovering His nature. Finally, the separation came to a close as Jesus hung on a cross and said, "It is finished!" (John 19:30). If God would go through all that trouble just to walk with us again, then the last thing He wants is a day away from us.

Remember, the Israelites disobeyed what God commanded them in the desert. Maybe it was fear of not having enough food, or maybe it was just plain laziness. Either way, they didn't heed God's instructions. Jesus tells us in Matthew 6:34 to let tomorrow worry about itself. These are wise words. God is willing and able to provide us with exactly what we need today. Please do not misunderstand me. I am not saying that we cannot use previous words or revelation from God. But it is very important that we remember what God has told us over the course of time. The testimonies of God's goodness are extremely powerful, and we are commissioned to continually tell them to those around us. I have also been given prophetic words from people that have not yet come to pass. Until they happen, I will continually keep them before me, fully trusting that God will do what He said. God may also have something for you today that you have yet to discover.

Listen for the Bread

When Satan tempted Jesus in the desert (Matt. 4), one of Satan's temptations was to turn some stones into bread. Jesus had been in the wilderness for 40 days. He was tired and hungry, and Satan came to him with bread. Jesus was fully capable of doing the very thing that Satan asked Him to do. Would it have been that big of a deal if Jesus had given in? What is so sinful about bread? Doesn't Jesus deserve a little bread after fasting for 40 days? But once again, there is amazing revelation underneath the phrases in the word that confuse us.

Jesus came back at the tempter with this statement: "Man shall not live on bread alone, but on every *word* that proceeds out of the mouth of God" (emphasis added) (Matt. 4:4). *Word* in this verse is the Greek word *rhema*, which means a spoken word or utterance. It is the same word used in Romans 10:17: "So faith comes from hearing, and hearing by the *word* of Christ" (emphasis added). *Rhema* is not necessarily a reference to the Bible here. Instead, it is referring to the very voice that God continues to speak today. Jesus is letting Satan know that the ability to hear from God the Father is the bread vital for His existence. Turning stones to bread may have been a good idea, but it wasn't a God idea. Jesus recognized that this particular request was birthed from the mind of the enemy rather than the mouth of God.

If we look closely, we will find some similarities and differences between Jesus in the wilderness and the Israelites in the wilderness. Both were stuck in a harsh environment, both were hungry, and both were given bread from above. But the outcomes of these accounts were completely different. The Israelites wandered in the wilderness for 40 years, and Jesus was led by the Holy Spirit in the desert for 40 days. Jesus defeated the enemy and thrived, but the Israelites gave in to temptations and died. When we are led by the voice of the Holy Spirit, our steps are directed and we move forward. However, without the leading of the Holy Spirit, all we can do is wander. If the Israelites had listened to the voice of God rather than the tempter, their journey in the wilderness would have taken only days rather than years.

Jesus never gave in to the enemy's tricks because He had ears to hear what His father was saying in every situation. His father's words spoken in a harsh environment were bread to Jesus's spirit and gave Him the ability to thrive in the presence of the devil himself.

But the Israelites didn't have the same relationship with God. In Chapter 3 of this book, we discovered that they only had access to what God said through what Moses told them. God wasn't personal to them. But Jesus had learned to cultivate a personal relationship with God the Father.

The response that Jesus gave Satan in Matthew 4:4 was a quote from the Old Testament.

> *You shall remember all the way which the LORD your God has led you in the wilderness these forty years, that He might humble you, testing you, to know what was in your heart, whether you would keep His commandments or not. He humbled you and let you be hungry, and fed you with manna which you did not know, nor did your fathers know, that He might make you understand that man does not live by bread alone, but man lives by everything that proceeds out of the mouth of the LORD.*
>
> —Deut. 8:2–3

God was teaching the Israelites an important lesson that they failed to realize. They continually complained about the situation they were in and were totally oblivious to what God wanted for their lives. His will was that they come out of the desert and into the promised land, but because of their unbelief due to their closed hearts, they perished in a land that wasn't made for them (Heb. 3:19). How are we just like them? Many of us continue in the desert far longer than we need to because we have stopped receiving direction from the Holy Spirit. What was meant to be only a transitional period becomes a life we are too familiar with. The wilderness was never meant to be the Israelites' home. It was meant to be a short, transitional journey to lead them to the land God had promised them. When you refuse to follow God's leading, what was meant to last only a few days turns into many years. It is important that we allow the Holy Spirit to lead us through the wilderness. Without the ability to hear from God, all we can do is wander around, lost in a land that isn't suited for living. If you inhabit the desert, you will never inherit the promise. Deserts only exist as transitional periods, not places where we are supposed to live our lives.

Unbelief Is Deaf

The people of Israel didn't have the faith to take the promised land because they couldn't hear the voice of God. Faith comes from hearing God's voice. When God speaks, my ears open. When my ears open, I can recognize His voice. When I recognize His voice, I can believe what He says. If you are unaware of the voice of God, then you won't be able to attain the measure of faith needed to take the things God has given you. The truth is, you can't enjoy what you are unaware of. Moses had extreme faith from meeting with God face-to-face, but the Israelites were not as fortunate. Their faith was absent because their ears were closed to what God was continually speaking. No matter the amazing miracles they witnessed, their faith remained withered. How is that possible? How could someone walk through parted waters yet lose faith in the one who parted them? Because the miracle was a thing of the past that couldn't empower them in their current troubles. Consistent faith doesn't come from a past miracle. It comes from God's daily bread. Faith comes from hearing, and hearing comes through the word of Christ (Romans 10:17). Miracles are amazing, but the purpose of a miracle is to point to the miracle maker.

Jesus got the nutrients He needed to thrive in the wilderness because He had cultivated a lifestyle of hearing from God the Father. He didn't rely on yesterday's supply; He ate of the bread His father gave Him daily. If we find ourselves in the wilderness, we have the ability to receive strength that will ultimately pull us out. It is when we stop listening to God's voice and start listening to the enemy's lies that we fall short of the land God has called us to inhabit. The enemy will always attempt to bring us his bread in tough times, but if we resist and remain faithful to God, then God's bread can move us out of the desert and into the places we desire. Do not lose heart in the dry, desert seasons. You were created to thrive in all circumstances.

The Author Speaks

Have you ever read the Bible and all of a sudden a verse jumped off the page, punched your spirit in the face, and filled you with encouragement? A little extreme, I know, but you get the picture. When I was reading Jeremiah 17 in my prayer closet, that very thing happened to me. Although they were verses I had heard before, they carried something different on that particular day. They brought new life and filled me with the hope I desperately needed in that moment. What was going on? The Holy Spirit was speaking to me. I believe that as we read God's supernatural, written word, the Holy Spirit takes specific verses and makes them jump off the page, so to speak, and become *rhema*. That is when what He has said in the past becomes what He is saying for the current situation. The entire Bible is inherently and completely good, but sometimes the Lord chooses to highlight certain verses that revive us and equip us for the current season and our present circumstances. When Jesus spoke to Satan, He was speaking the scriptures that He had read all His life. But because it was useful for His current situation, it became *rhema*, the spoken word of God.

In those days, the only Bible they had was the Old Testament, and Jesus knew it well. It wasn't neatly compiled in one place like the Bibles we have today but was written in scrolls with no chapters or verses. Jesus spent His life developing a relationship with God the Father through daily readings of these scrolls and through prayer. When Jesus went out to the desert to be tempted by Satan, it was unlikely that He was carrying scrolls with Him. But it didn't matter. The words He once read now became part of Him and the words He could now speak. He was able to speak scripture against Satan, not because He had it in front of Him but because He had it within Him. As we read God's written word, it becomes a part of us, and then we can speak it against anything that comes against us. Not only can we hear a *rhema* from God, but we can also speak a *rhema* into the world around us. We speak the words we read in His book. God is calling each of us to be a mouthpiece for His goodness in this life.

As Christians, we should keep a healthy balance between listening to what God is saying and reading what He has already said. One doesn't replace the other. If we have eyes to see but no ears to hear, we will miss God's complete direction for our lives. That was the Pharisees' problem. They read the pages but couldn't hear the author.

How Does God Speak?

How does God speak? Can I truly hear His voice? These are questions I have asked myself over the years as I walked as a Christian. Sadly, many people are asking these same questions. Too often, we walk through life thinking we are incapable of hearing our Lord. However, the Bible makes a distinct promise that completely shatters this idea.

> *To him the doorkeeper opens, and the sheep hear his voice, and he calls his own sheep by name and leads them out. When he puts forth all his own, he goes ahead of them, and the sheep follow him because they know his voice. A stranger they simply will not follow, but will flee from him, because they do not know the voice of strangers.*
>
> *—John 10:3–5*

These verses make one bold promise. It is a God-given ability within all believers to hear His voice. Regardless of feelings or circumstance, you have been given the capacity to hear heaven's call. Each of us has unlimited access to the voice of God. "The sheep follow him because they know his voice" (John 10:4). One of the enemy's main tactics is to trick you into believing you have issues with hearing. If he can stifle God's voice, he can then keep you from walking in God's purpose. The good news is that he can't actually keep God from speaking. He is an illusionist instilling lies in your head that manifest in your life. The belief that you can't hear is the only thing hindering you from hearing. Once you come to the conclusion that you were built to hear, a door is opened that seemed to have previously been shut tightly.

Many confine the voice of God to just one or maybe two ways of speaking. In doing so, they have silenced many of the auditory avenues through which He has chosen to communicate. There are truly no limits to how God can communicate with His kids. I have found eight ways that God uses His voice to communicate with people. Let me show you in the following pages using the acronym HISVOICE.

HISVOICE

1. Hearing audibly
Although I have never experienced this particular way of communication, I have read it in God's word and heard testimonies from other believers. God the Father spoke audibly to Jesus when He was baptized in the Jordan River. After Jesus ascended to heaven, He spoke to Paul audibly as he was traveling to Damascus. Although this way of communication is quite rare, it is unwise to eliminate it altogether.

2. *Internal knowings*

I like to think of these as thoughts. They seem to be the most prevalent in my life. God often drops thoughts in my mind about various things throughout the day. Sometimes it is a revelatory one-line statement regarding scripture that brings understanding to what was previously confusing. Sometimes it's a word of knowledge about someone else, which opens a door for gospel-centered conversation. It can even be a simple yes or no answer to a question I asked Him. Regardless, God often speaks to the minds of believers. After all, we have been given the mind of Christ (1 Cor. 2:16).

3. *Scripture*

No one is debating whether or not God speaks through scripture. Sadly, many brothers and sisters in Christ have restricted His voice to the Bible only. Although He does speak through His written word, He is not confined to what He wrote. If the Bible is His only way of communication, then how will we know whom to marry, what job to seek, what school to attend, or what town to reside in? However, God will never speak something that contradicts what He has already written. If the voice you listen to contradicts the Bible you hold, you are listening to the wrong voice. As we read the word, God illuminates our understanding of reality and allows us to see as He sees. Those who don't read the Bible miss out on many of the answers they are seeking in life.

4. *Visions and Dreams*

> *Indeed God speaks once,*
> *Or twice, yet no one notices it.*
> *In a dream, a vision of the night,*
> *When sound sleep falls on men,*
> *While they slumber in their beds,*
> *Then He opens the ears of men,*
> *And seals their instruction.*

> *—Job 33:14–16*

99

Many people have experienced the voice of God in their dreams. Although our dreams are often a result of our poor meal choices, God is still willing and able to encounter us in the night. Visions can also come in the form of mental pictures. There are even such things as "open visions" where God gives people access to see into the spiritual realm here on earth. I know a lady who actually sees different colors over people that are hidden from the normal eye. She actually predicted our son before we knew he was coming simply because she saw the color blue over my wife!

5. Other people

God often speaks to a person through another person. This is the beauty of prophetic insight. God has often given me a word He wanted me to deliver to someone. Likewise, I have received many words from others that were straight from God. It is a wonderful opportunity to become a mouthpiece for the Lord. Have I received bad words before? Absolutely! But rather than stifle the voice entirely, I simply take personal responsibility to decipher between truth and lie. I would submit that there are daily opportunities for you to deliver a message from heaven to someone you encounter.

6. Impressions

I think of impressions as feelings. Although we shouldn't let every feeling lead our lives, to avoid them altogether is problematic. Even God has feelings. I have often been given a deep impression to do something that I later realized was completely from the Lord. It can be the impression to take a different route home, to call a friend, to pursue a specific career, or to say yes or no to a major life decision. Don't deny your feelings; become aware of them. They could very well be the voice of God.

7. *Creation*

> *For since the creation of the world His invisible attributes, His eternal power and divine nature, have been clearly seen, being understood through what has been made, so that they are without excuse.*

—*Rom. 1:20*

God is clearly seen in His creation. He is the artist who signs each of His paintings. Everything that is visible holds within in it a little piece of His divine nature. His voice radiates throughout the universe through all He has crafted. The sunset that inspires creativity, the mountain that ignites awe, and the unique animal that unravels wonder—all have become a storyteller of the majesty of God. I had a God encounter on my honeymoon, sitting on the back porch of a rented cabin in the middle of the Smoky Mountains as I stared at a majestic mountain in front of me. Look around. He is everywhere.

8. *Everything*

Communicating through everything may seem like a complete cop-out, but hear me out. I have included it just to keep you from creating another confining religious list. God has no communication limits. When we limit His voice, we also limit our future. My abundant future is contingent upon His eternal voice. Abundance without His voice becomes a curse rather than a blessing. God can speak through anything, anywhere, anytime. Whether it is a song on the radio, a news reporter on TV, or even a shirt your friend is wearing, there truly are no limits.

When we discover that God is always speaking and that we have been invited into the conversation, it allows us to walk with full assurance that we are headed in the right direction. Jesus modeled this when He said that He only says what God the Father tells Him to say (John 12:49). God is in constant communication with us. Look around and hear His voice. It's your God-given right.

Formula-Free

Jesus made it a priority to meet with His heavenly father daily. It wasn't just a good idea; it was the very thing that gave Him the strength and courage to take the next step on His journey. Before and after every major event, He drew away from the massive crowds and His friends to seek the Lord in prayer (Luke 5:16). The supernatural life He lived came out of His constant conversation with the father. Even before the Lord of glory was crucified, He spent the previous night talking to His father and getting His perspective. It is in the alone times with God that we can rest and hear His voice. Those who get burned out and become extremely discouraged in their walk are usually those who have stopped meeting with God the Father daily.

On the other hand, many have taken this idea of personal prayer time and created a religious formula out of it, meeting God only at specified times. While God does want time alone with you, He also doesn't want to be distant during our daily activities. God is still present in the mundane. Paul wrote in 1 Thessalonians 5:17 that we should pray without ceasing. How is that possible? Does that look like a life of complete seclusion that only involves a never-ending verbal conversation with God, void of any other relationships? That sounds awful. I would submit that Paul's point is that every second of the day can hold an awareness of His presence. Life is not about eternal seclusion in an effort to connect with the Lord. It is about walking through the tasks of our daily lives with Him. He wants to be part of our entire walk, not just the moments we carve out for Him. Prayer without ceasing looks like a continual awareness of His presence.

Jesus did a lot of healing in the four Gospels. He raised the dead, restored sight to the blind, removed demons, restored limbs, and much more. But what is interesting is that Jesus didn't create a formula for healing certain diseases. Each healing looked a little different than the last. Often Christians find something that works well and create programs and formulas in which they become confident. But the problem we often encounter is that we become so comfortable in our programs that we stop listening to Him for new ways to do things. Religion creates formulas, but relationship remains attentive and obedient. Many churches have fallen into this trap. They are so set in their programs and procedures that anything that looks a little bit different is immediately thrown to the curb. I'm not talking about sacrificing the gospel for a new one or replacing Christian doctrine for New Age jargon. What I am saying is that God may have new ways of doing old things. God is creative, and He has given His children that same creativity. He wants us to constantly listen to His voice so we can create and release new things in the world around us. The next billion-dollar idea could start as a small request that God gives you.

Jesus made this statement to a group of Jews who were accusing Him:

> *Truly, truly, I say to you, the Son can do nothing of Himself, unless it is something He sees the Father doing; for whatever the Father does, these things the Son also does in like manner.*
>
> —*John 5:19*

Before Jesus ever did anything, He first had to see His father doing it. He didn't come to a point in His ministry where He relied on healing formulas from the past. He always received His father's perspective before He healed anyone. If Jesus relied on His father's direction every moment of His ministry, why should I be any different? Some of us haven't seen any breakthroughs in certain areas of our lives because we are trying old things that once worked but now have no effect. Too often, we replace the God who speaks for a formula that once worked. God doesn't want to sacrifice a listening child for a step-by-step formula. If we continue to listen to the voice of God, we will receive new ideas, fresh revelation, and much needed encouragement to take the next step.

What He gave me yesterday was wonderful, and I may never forget it. But rather than avoid Him today because I have yesterday's spiritual food in the fridge, I will make it a priority to live with God the Father daily and receive from Him. After all, today is a new day, and yesterday is just a memory.

8

Created to Release

There is one kingdom truth that has often been misunderstood in the church. If not misunderstood, it has simply been devalued. Whether misunderstood or devalued, the outcome remains the same—a group of believers who aren't walking in the fullness of an aspect of the kingdom, the aspect that Jesus died for us to not only walk in but also understand. I am talking about worship. For me, understanding true worship is vital in the life of a believer. To understand the importance of worship is to understand a necessary part of your divinely created purpose. If we truly want to thrive in all circumstances, this topic cannot be overlooked. We were created to worship. The pages in this chapter come from my personal journey of uncovering God's heart.

I grew up in church. Whether I wanted to go or not was irrelevant. My mom did a great job of making sure I attended Sunday school and learned about Jesus. It was (and still is) of high value in her life. Although I look back and remember my annoyance with church, I am extremely grateful for my upbringing. It is because of her that I carried into my adulthood a knowledge of biblical characters and the gospel of Christ.

During that time in my life, I established belief systems that would forever change the way I viewed the world around me. Some were true and still exist today; some were false, and the Lord has been successfully cutting those away since I became serious about following Him. It is so with every human. Each of us has ways of thinking that we pick up in life that either help us or hurt us. One negative belief I carried with me was on the subject of worship.

I thought worship was simply a tiny little time slot before and after the sermon when we would pull out our hymn books and sing. But is worship just singing or music? Whether your church sings a cappella, uses hymn books, or has a full band with a light show is irrelevant. Worship may include these physical elements and expressions, but it is not defined by them. If we dumb down our worship to just singing or music, we rob it of its true beauty and purpose. Worship is actually much deeper than what is visible.

To understand worship as a time slot once or twice a week is to have an event-based mentality of worship. The problem with event-based worship is that it is temporary. We worship and then must wait an entire week to rejoin our fellow Christian brothers and sisters to engage in worship again. That tells me that worship is not something that is relevant to daily living and is something that is only active at certain times within the four walls of a church building. Don't get me wrong, I absolutely love singing to God with my church family on Sundays. Being a worship leader in the local church has developed within me a high value for those times. It is, in fact, my favorite part of a service. Even so, I have realized that worship is far more than our set-aside music moments. The truth is that worship is not an event; it is a lifestyle.

Worship Revealed

Let's go back to John 4 where Jesus was having a conversation with the Samaritan woman at a well. After He speaks with her about the living water of the Holy Spirit He was going to pour out, He asks her to go get her husband. Surprised by such a question, she responds, "I have no husband" (John 4:17). It was at that moment that Jesus agreed with her and began to call her out. He said to her, "You have correctly said, 'I have no husband'; for you have had five husbands, and the one whom you now have is not your husband; this you have said truly" (John 4:17–18). Imagine her thought process. A random guy with odd language and supernatural insight just called out the secret sin in her life. Who does He think He is? What is His business in my business? She did what she knew to do: deflect and change the subject.

She began to ask Jesus a question about worship. Although her question was rooted in the fear of her own sin and the appearance of sounding spiritual, Jesus decided to indulge her and give her what, I think, is the greatest revelation on the subject of worship. Let's look at her question.

> *Our fathers worshiped in this mountain, and you people say that in Jerusalem is the place where men ought to worship.*
>
> —*John 4:20*

Notice how her focus was the *place*. She was asking Jesus where the designated place of worship was. Presented with only two options—the mountain or Jerusalem—Jesus was put on the spot. But rather than answer with A or B, He responds to her question with a no. Jesus said to her, "Woman, believe Me, an hour is coming when neither in this mountain nor in Jerusalem will you worship the Father" (John 4:21). What is He trying to say? Is He about to provide her with a physical place that she hadn't thought of? Her question is one we can relate to today.

Many are in the same boat wondering where the perfect place to worship is. Is it in the church building with an amazing worship team? Is it in the car with the radio blaring? Is it in the shower when the acoustics are just right and our voice sounds angelic? The answer is no. Jesus is actually revealing that worship is not a designated place to visit. It is not a specific action at a specific location. So often we pair worship with a church service or a destination, but worship is not an event that happens in a specific place. It is a lifestyle. Its purpose is to be released in every area of life. I believe God is looking for people who aren't looking for the right place or chasing down conferences and services. He is looking for people who are continually living in His presence.

The Place of Worship

To attempt to fully define worship is to embark on a lifelong journey. Worship is such a deep, rich subject that we will continually be unraveling it until the triumphant return of Jesus. I have received an understanding that has forever changed the way I view worship. I will run through several definitions that I believe best support my current revelation. But before we cover *what* worship is, it is important to realize *where* worship begins. The truth is, worship starts in the heart.

I am not talking about the organ that pumps blood through our bodies, but rather the place from whence love flows, where we feel and experience the world around us. Worship is birthed there. My favorite definition of worship comes from Dan McCollum, minister and founding director of Sounds of the Nations, who says that worship is not a song that is sung but a heart that sings. It is truly a heart issue. Paul reinforces this idea in his letter to the Ephesians.

And do not get drunk with wine, for that is dissipation, but be filled with the Spirit, speaking to one another in psalms and hymns and spiritual songs, singing and making melody with your heart to the Lord.

—Eph. 5:18–19

What is the song of your heart? Is it a melody unto the Lord? Every church has a time, usually before the message, that involves singing. For me, this once encompassed the entirety of what worship was, but it is actually just an expression of worship. These times of singing can be beautiful and pleasing to the Lord unless the heart is not in it. Singing words projected on a screen without a heart that is turned to the Lord is not true worship. It's karaoke. Yes, singing songs to God is extremely important in a believer's life. Throughout the Bible are examples of praising and worshiping God through voice and music, and I do not want to diminish that. But God is more interested in the song of your heart than the sound of your voice. Actually, true worship flows from a postured heart.

What is a postured heart? In Psalm 119:7, the author writes, "I will praise you with an upright heart, when I learn of your righteous rules" (ESV). There are seven distinctive Hebrew words that are translated *praise* in the English Bible. It is interesting that all seven words are action words, or verbs. The Hebrew word for *praise* in the above verse is *yadah*, which means "to lift the hands." If we placed that definition into this verse, it would read like this: "I will lift my hands to you with an upright heart." Now we can see that the action of praise is actually coming from the heart. Notice how it is not just a heart but an *upright* heart. What is upright? It is a posture. When a heart is turned toward the Lord, it seems to be considered upright. I believe that every action of praise comes from a heart that is properly postured toward the Lord. In essence, praise flows from a heart of worship. Actions of praise are limitless. Shouting, dancing, singing, lifting hands, painting, and playing music are just a few. Truly, any action can be praise to God.

Let's look at the differences between praise and worship. I know I run the risk of over-reducing these spiritual concepts, but I will do the best I can to simplify them without removing their weight and mystery. As we've seen, praise is always action. Worship, however, is more. Anything birthed from the heart is worship, not just physical expression. That includes thoughts, emotions, and other unseen objects. Worship is a heart posture, and praise is the action that flows from it. Praise is confined to action, but everything is worship.

It is only when the heart is properly postured that our worship becomes genuine. Anyone can fake a motion, but it takes a heart of worship to produce pure praise. To run through the motions but not acknowledge whom it is all for is to re-create a religious formula that is void of God. God's heart is to see His children respond to His goodness, not to just follow a powerless pattern. I don't have to teach my son to be excited about bath time. He just has a personal understanding of a bath's goodness and naturally releases a genuine expression. Worship is like that. We understand how good God is, and then release a genuine expression with a properly postured heart.

So where is the place of worship? The place of worship is in our hearts. When the Samaritan woman asked Jesus where the perfect worship spot was, she was thinking in the context of her tradition. Her tradition taught that worship only took place in the temple. In the Old Testament, human hands built a temple where God could dwell and people could visit. Yet as we have discussed several times in this book, believers are now the temple of God. We no longer have to visit a place to worship; we are the place of worship. Therefore, everywhere I go, I worship.

The True Worshipers

As Jesus continued his conversation with the woman at the well, He began to describe a certain group of people God the Father was searching for. It was a group of people who could change the world around them by what they released from within them.

But an hour is coming, and now is, when the true worshipers will worship the Father in spirit and truth; for such people the Father seeks to be His worshipers.

—John 4:23

In this verse, Jesus takes the focus off the place and draws attention to the people. This is crucial for us to see and understand. If I believe God is only looking for worship, in my mind, He becomes egotistical and needy. I have the potential to see Him as a selfish being who doesn't care about anything other than receiving what He wants from us. However, if I understand that God is looking for worshipers, not just worship, He moves from egotistical to relational. God the Father doesn't want His children lifting up praise just for the sake of praise. That mentality paints a picture of God as a weary worker who is ready to cast His résumé into another universe unless he gets some sort of affirmation for his efforts. The truth is, He wants relational connections. If I am worshiping, I am connecting.

Before Jesus mentioned the true worshipers to this woman, He made an interesting comment. "You worship what you do not know; we worship what we know, for salvation is from the Jews" (John 4:22). This is a simple verse that can often get overlooked. I believe, Jesus is getting to the root of worship in this verse. He claims there are many people who are attempting to worship a God they don't truly know. That's when worship becomes powerless and pointless. Why would someone worship a God they don't know? Because they are following a tradition instead of the trinity. I can recall moments in a church service when I held my hymn book and sang words I didn't understand or even care to understand. I wasn't worshiping God. I was reciting a poem to music. The purpose of worship is relational connection. True, I'm giving Him glory, honor, and praise because He deserves it. However, I am doing so out of love instead of tradition. Jesus said, "We worship what we know." True worship will inevitably happen when we understand who God is. If we witness His majesty and beauty, we are compelled to truly worship. I can't sit still passively if I see Him for who He is. Neither can I partake in meaningless traditional motions.

There is an eye-opening verse in Amos 5 in which God is speaking.

I hate, I reject your festivals,
Nor do I delight in your solemn assemblies.
Even though you offer up to Me burnt offerings
and your grain offerings,
I will not accept them;
And I will not even look at the peace offerings of your fatlings.
Take away from Me the noise of your songs;
I will not even listen to the sound of your harps.
But let justice roll down like waters
And righteousness like an ever-flowing stream.

—Amos 5:21–24

Here is an example of the kind of worship God hates: anything not birthed from a love of Him; any act of worship that is merely traditional instead of relational, exactly the opposite of what God wants to receive. This verse explicitly proves that God doesn't want worship. He wants worshipers, people who continually give Him glory from the overflow of their hearts. God doesn't need your worship. He wants your heart. We must mentally return to His original design for worship—to connect with His kids. Yes, He is holy. Yes, He commands worship. But I don't do it because I'm commanded to. I do it because I love God.

We see another example in what Jesus said to the Pharisees, quoting the prophet Isaiah:

THIS PEOPLE HONORS ME WITH THEIR LIPS,
BUT THEIR HEART IS FAR FROM ME.
BUT IN VAIN DO THEY WORSHIP ME,
TEACHING AS DOCTRINES THE PRECEPTS OF MEN.

—Matt. 15:8–9

Again, we clearly see the purpose of worship: to offer up the overflow of our hearts. King David was a worshiper who was called a man after God's own heart. Truly, worship is a person's heart pursuing the heart of God. I love; therefore, I worship.

There are really only two kinds of worship: true and false. How do you know what kind of worship yours is? It is defined by where it is directed. When your worship is aimed at anything other than God the Father, it becomes meaningless and unfulfilling.

Worshiper by Nature

Every person on this planet is a worshiper by nature. It was written in your blueprint before the foundation of the world and built into your being the minute we were born. We can't escape it. It is, in fact, a hardwired need in us all. We must worship something. The question is not will I worship but rather what will I worship?

If God is not the target of my worship, I will spend my life chasing down temporary objects in an effort to give them what they weren't created for. I must release my worship, but to do so toward a part of His creation is misdirected. You see this often in sports fans. I am not saying that being a sports fan is bad, but there is a point when it can become unhealthy. If the outcome of a specific game determines how you will treat your family for the week, it is evident that you have misdirected your worship. Instead of simply being a sport to enjoy, it has become the idol you depend on. You begin to live in response to your team. Or take for instance a young newlywed. The moment their partner becomes their idol, the relationship becomes unhealthy. They start to expect things that their mate cannot provide, resulting in an unsatisfied marriage and, if the marriage is not healed, a permanent separation. In either one of these examples the point remains the same. These objects of worship change. Teams trade players and hire new coaches. Partners have whimsical emotions and fluctuating opinions. The only thing that will never change is the character and nature of God. He is the only constant. When I choose to worship Him, I am satisfied every time.

Worship is a 24/7 job that lasts a lifetime. The tabernacle in King David's time was known for having 24/7 worship with singers and musicians. Today, many people are attempting to replicate that model in their churches and ministries with nonstop worship music. I would never say this is bad. I will completely jump on board with those who are making melodies to God every second of the day. The problem is that it isn't sustainable in everyday life. Maybe the tabernacle isn't necessarily the pinnacle level of worship. I happen to believe it is the old covenant symbol for the new covenant lifestyle of worship. In other words, we supersede the tabernacle because we are the temple of God. I am His temple because He lives within me. Wherever I go, worship happens 24/7.

A God of Gold

There is an interesting story in Exodus 32 that many Christians have become familiar with. It is another one of those cute Bible stories we learned as kids. You more than likely know it as the story of the golden calf. I found reading this story as an adult to be quite entertaining and humorous. I challenge you to reread the Bible stories you heard at a young age and see how different they are now. The story of Noah and the ark has been depicted as a nice little story of a floating zoo and a rainbow. In reality, every animal and human outside the confines of Noah's boat died a horribly painful death. But I digress.

I touched on the Exodus 32 passage briefly in Chapter 4, but let's take a deeper dive and see if we can find some pure gold. In this chapter, Moses is on Mount Sinai, and the Israelites are growing impatient. He had been gone for 40 days, and the Israelites assumed he wasn't coming back. They approached Aaron, Moses's brother and right-hand man, and asked him to make a new god to go before them. Aaron told the people to bring him all their gold jewelry. I guess he had temporarily forgotten who the one true God was. After he had collected all their gold jewelry, he melted them down and then molded it into the shape of a calf. I wonder if Aaron was a skilled craftsman. For all we know, it could have been the world's worst representation of a heifer. Then Aaron introduced the Israelites to their new god, and they began to worship it and bring sacrifices to it. We read this and think it is irrelevant in today's culture. We can't fathom bowing down to a golden calf. But this happens more often than we realize. The truth is that since the beginning, people have allowed human-made objects to take God's place.

When all this was taking place, God's words were ringing out on top of the mountain as Moses listened. Knowing what was going on at the bottom of the mountain at the Israelites' camp, God told Moses of His plan to smite them. Oddly enough, Moses finds himself in a heated discussion that ultimately changes God's mind about wiping out His people. That part of the Bible hurts my analytical mind and theological stance. How could a human change God's mind? I don't know, but it's those verses that keep me coming back for more as I beg the Holy Spirit for a deeper understanding of God's word.

Once Moses had successfully persuaded God, he traveled down the mountain, carrying with him the two tablets of stone with the ten commandments engraved on them by the finger of God. When Moses arrived at the camp, the horrific images of his people singing and dancing around a golden calf pierced his eyes. With a deep sense of anger and betrayal, he threw down God's tablets and proceeded to destroy their new god. The Bible says he burned it, ground it into powder, scattered it into the water, and made them drink it. Moses was a very influential man to have the authority to make all those people drink gold-powdered water, but it also sends a humorous message. Idols probably taste terrible.

Although worshiping something created may have its temporary benefits and contain a level of fun, in the long run, the taste is bitter and harmful to the body. There is only one who is able to satisfy our hearts' craving. "O taste and see that the LORD is good; How blessed is the man who takes refuge in Him!" (Ps. 34:8) He is the only one who fits that spot. We are not forced into a religion void of encounters. We are invited to experience Him through every physical sense, not just knowing about Him.

Moses eventually asked Aaron how he had allowed the people to persuade him to create such an idol. Reading Aaron's response makes me laugh every time. He said, "I threw it [the jewelry] into the fire, and out came this calf" (Exod. 32:24). That was his best response. To me, it sounds more like a child's response to cover up a wrong decision. I'm sure Aaron knew that what he was doing was wrong, yet he allowed the people around him to dictate how he would live. Had Aaron stood up for who he knew to be the Lord, maybe this story would have ended a little better. There will always be voices attempting to pull you away from the God who has shown Himself to you. Stand firm and remember who He is.

When we see God as a distant being, we limit what we can experience. We begin to run after the things we can touch, not realizing He is more tangible than we know. He is a God of intimacy and love. As I experience more of His life-giving power, I am compelled to leave the viewing room and jump into the center of His heart.

A Lifestyle of Worship

Returning to my original point, worship is a lifestyle. It is a beautiful moment when a Christian discovers that everything he or she does is worship—from eating breakfast to the responsibilities we have at work, and everything in between. Even the most unspiritual sounding things in life have their own weight of glory.

The apostle Paul was an example of a worshiping lifestyle. It was said that people would take aprons and handkerchiefs that had come in contact with his skin, lay them on the sick and demon-possessed, and see them completely healed (Acts 19:12). How was that possible? Did Paul spend hours praying over these cloths? I highly doubt it. Those who seek to replicate this have missed the point entirely. These were simply aprons that would keep dirt off of him and handkerchiefs he would use to wipe his brow on a long workday. Paul was a tentmaker by trade. The work he accomplished that seemed so unspiritual still contained the anointing within it to the heal sick. How? Because everything is worship. This is only possible for people who know who they are and knows who He is.

Worship begins when you awake every morning and become conscious of your surroundings. It is impossible to worship what does not have your attention. True worship is a continuous awareness of the goodness of God. With this awareness, everything you do gives Him glory. Don't be fooled into believing that worship only happens when the church music starts. That is a beautiful and necessary form of worship but cannot become the box that confines it. True worship begins within, and there, every song, every shout, and every action is born.

Just as a tree releases oxygen, you release worship. It's who you are: a worshiper. You are a mighty tree rooted in the rivers of God to release worship into the atmosphere around you, positively influencing the world and giving glory to its creator. Wake up every morning with an awareness of His goodness, and everything you do will be praise and worship to Him. Go ahead. Release what you were created for.

9

Inside the Unseen

Heaven is a reality that Christians know exists. Oddly enough, we have never been there or seen it. We believe that we will go there one day, but right now it remains unseen. It has the characteristics of the wind. We feel it and see its physical effects, yet it remains invisible. We know Paul was called up to the third heaven, and we continually hear many claims, whether true or false, of people visiting heaven and returning to give us a glimpse. So what exactly is heaven? Better yet, where is heaven?

Uncontainable

Heaven has commonly been described as the place where God lives. While I do see the logic in that, I also recognize an error. If God is everlasting and never ending, then it is impossible for Him to be confined to one location, even if that location is considered to be limitless. The moment He is confined to a place, He ceases to be God. All of this can be remedied with a new understanding of heaven. God is not in heaven; heaven is in God. Heaven is not simply a place where God lives; it is a life within Him. Everything that could ever be and has ever been is contained within Him.

He is the image of the invisible God, the firstborn of all creation. For by Him all things were created, both in the heavens and on earth, visible

119

and invisible, whether thrones or dominions or rulers or authorities—all things have been created through Him and for Him. He is before all things, and in Him all things hold together.

—Col. 1:15–17

These verses speak of Christ. Notice how it says "in Him all things hold together." Heaven is a limitless world located within our limitless Lord. It stretches as far as the eternal God yet is contained within His uncontainable being.

King Solomon had this same understanding of God's uncontainable being when He spoke in 1 Kings 8:27 regarding the temple he made for God: "But will God indeed dwell on the earth? Behold, heaven and the highest heaven cannot contain You, how much less this house which I have built!" Solomon understood that nothing is bigger or greater than the God he knew.

John Gill, a Baptist theologian, wrote in the 1700s about this verse in his *Exposition of the Entire Bible.*

Behold, the heaven, and the heaven of heavens, cannot contain thee; not only the visible heavens, but the third heaven, where the throne of God is, and is the habitation of angels and saints; though there God makes the most glorious displays of himself yet he is so immense and infinite, that he is not to be comprehended and circumscribed in any place whatever.[1]

And so we are met with a paradox. God is so big that heaven can't contain Him, yet He is so personal that He dwells within me. This is the glory of God. He is creator of everything ever created, but in the person of Jesus, He put on skin and came to earth to meet us face-to-face. The builder decided to step in and see his work close up.

More Than a Place

Heaven is more than a place or a destination. It is a way of life—God's way of life, the abundant life. Jesus uses the term *kingdom of heaven* many times in the Gospels. The term is also synonymous with kingdom of God. A kingdom at that time was not merely a walled city but also a way of life. Much like the nation you reside in, there is a certain way of doing things.

Too often Christians view heaven as merely the destination for the righteous. Many conjure up visions of mansions, cars, and cash and claim that acquiring a vast amount of useless objects is the pinnacle of life. Therefore, heaven becomes the destination where all your earthly dreams come true. For many, Jesus is absent in their picture of the afterlife. However, I believe that heaven without Jesus is not heaven at all. In John 14:6, Jesus says that He is the life. Any life lived apart from Jesus is not a life worth living. Jesus is not a means to an end. He is the beginning and the end, the alpha and the omega. Heaven is being with Jesus. This truly is the only thing that will bring sustainable, never-ending fulfillment.

Yet there is an amount of heaven that is to be experienced in this life. Heaven is not just an after-death experience; it is also a right-now reality. We briefly looked at this in Chapter 6 when we examined the Lord's Prayer. "Your kingdom come. Your will be done, On earth as it is in heaven" (Matt. 6:10). God's will is that we would bring the unseen realities of heaven to our observable environment. Although the fullness of heaven will not be discovered until the Second Coming of Christ, we are still able to witness a portion of it in this life.

In Luke 10, Jesus sent out 70 disciples to go before Him into various cities He was planning to visit. He gave them specific instructions, describing what to do when a city accepts them. Then He said, "And heal those in it who are sick, and say to them, 'The kingdom of God has come near to you'" (Luke 10:9). How did the kingdom come near to them? Because heaven is more than a place; it is a way of life. These 70 disciples were invited by Jesus to walk on earth, demonstrating the supernatural ways of the kingdom. Miracles occur when the unseen kingdom of heaven collides with this physical world.

Jesus has extended the same invitation to us today:

Go into all the world and preach the gospel to all creation. He who has believed and has been baptized shall be saved; but he who has disbelieved shall be condemned. These signs will accompany those who have believed: in My name they will cast out demons, they will speak with new tongues; they will pick up serpents, and if they drink any deadly poison, it will not hurt them; they will lay hands on the sick, and they will recover.

—Mark 16:15–18

As a Christian, you have been commissioned to demonstrate the impossible. If your life isn't supernatural, you are living well below your Christ-like capabilities. He has delegated His authority and power to you as a child of God. Don't wait until you die to live a supernatural life. Accept His commission and release the wonder of the kingdom to everything you come in contact with. Yes, heaven is a limitless world, but it is also an abundant lifestyle.

Thieves

The kingdom of heaven is a way of life and the highest possible level of living. There are kingdom culture and kingdom principles that are to be adopted by the believer and demonstrated to the world. We are not confined to the cage of natural thinking and living; we have been called to see as He sees and live as He lives. We are, after all, the king's kids, wrapped in His royalty.

Yet, when we look at the world today, we find kingdom principles being used by those who do not know the king yet. The New Age movement is a prime example. Those associated with it preach faith, positive thinking, prayer, meditation, and miracles along with many other things that have their roots in the Bible. A vast number of people have become fearful of core Christian beliefs, simply because they are being accepted by the wrong group. But rather than be afraid of them, we need to know where their teachings originated. They have stolen a handful of biblical truths, removed Jesus, and repackaged them. It often sounds good and feels Christian, but underneath, it has been stripped of all power.

In the Gospel of John, Jesus makes this statement to a group of Pharisees: "Truly, truly, I say to you, he who does not enter by the door into the fold of the sheep, but climbs up some other way, he is a thief and a robber" (John 10:1). In the context, the sheep Jesus is referring to are His followers. He is declaring that anyone who doesn't go through the door to get to the gathered sheep, or kingdom, is a thief. If someone chooses to enter the kingdom without going through Christ, he is trespassing. That tells me several things.

First, it is possible for non-Christians to experience a portion of the kingdom, although obviously not in its fullness. The Bible explicitly describes the outcome for those who do not believe in Christ's finished work. Even believers will not see the kingdom in its entirety until the return of Christ. But in this life, there is a piece of God's world that anyone is able to experience.

Second, non-Christians can use biblical principles that will help them in this life. Take, for instance, the subject of tithing, a principle that all sons and daughters of God are invited to take part in. It is a beautiful expression of trusting God with our finances. To top it off, God tells us He will bless those who give generously. This, however, isn't the purpose of tithing. It is only the side effect. I tithe because I love and trust Him, not because I want something from Him. Even so, there are unbelievers who have grasped the concept of financial generosity and are seeing an increase in their lives because of it. What has happened? They have hijacked God's word and used it for personal gain.

Jesus refers to the one navigating around Him, using His ways as a thief. But Jesus regards His sheep as those who have entered through Him. It is like the one who sneaked into the movie theater without paying compared to the one who actually bought a ticket. The reality is, Jesus already purchased your ticket to enter heaven's theater. Those who are trying so hard to sneak into heaven fail to realize that it is a free gift to anyone who will simply come to Jesus. There is no striving involved, just simple surrender.

Jesus continued His conversation with the Pharisees:

> *But he who enters by the door is a shepherd of the sheep. To him the doorkeeper opens, and the sheep hear his voice, and he calls his own sheep by name and leads them out. When he puts forth all his own, he goes ahead of them, and the sheep follow him because they know his voice.*
>
> *—John 10:2–4*

I love the magnitude of Christ depicted here. He says He is the door, the gatekeeper, the shepherd. And notice that He goes ahead of the sheep. Once we enter through Him, we are not left to figure everything out on our own. He actually leads us while showing us how life operates in His world. Thieves may have the ability to steal a few things, but they will never be given a grand tour from the king of kings.

Compare this to my backyard. It is a private area behind my house surrounded by a fence. I have tools, toys, and many other items organized back there. If it's in my yard, it belongs to me. There are only two ways you can use what I own. Either I let you in and show you where it is, or you hop my fence and take it without permission.

So it is with Jesus. He has given all believers access to His yard, or heaven. He also shows us how everything operates there. The best news is that when Jesus gives us access, it actually becomes ours. We are no longer standing in His yard; we are standing in our yard. Heaven becomes our home. We are not visitors; we are residents.

If I skip down a few verses in Jesus's conversation with the Pharisees, I find a foundational verse for me as well as the church in which I serve. It says, "The thief comes only to steal and kill and destroy; I came that they may have life, and have it abundantly (John 10:10). The first thing to realize is the separation between God's will and the thief's will. If whatever you are experiencing in your life fits under the category of steal, kill, or destroy, it cannot be attributed to God. The thief that is described in this verse is commonly a reference to Satan. Although I believe this is true, it is only true in part. Due to the context of these verses, Jesus is not only referring to Satan but to anyone who tries to climb into the kingdom by avoiding Him. If someone hops my backyard fence, they are there for one of three reasons: to steal something, to kill someone, or to destroy something. There are no other options.

We have no reason to fear what unbelievers are using from the kingdom. They may be able to experience God's goodness in part, but they will never know the fullness of the truth they are using. As we walk on this earth in a heavenly way, we are demonstrating the abundant life to everyone we encounter. People will see our physical blessings, but it is the unseen, invisible relationship we have with God that will keep them pondering who we are and enticing them to meet this Jesus for themselves. From there, they will be able to become co-owners of the very thing they once stole from God's world.

Planted in Heaven

We are considered citizens of heaven, not one day, but right now in this life. We currently have access to the never-ending abundance of heaven because we are placed right in the middle of it.

> *But God, being rich in mercy, because of His great love with which He loved us, even when we were dead in our transgressions, made us alive together with Christ (by grace you have been saved), and raised us up with Him, **and seated us with Him in the heavenly places in Christ Jesus**, so that in the ages to come He might show the surpassing riches of His grace in kindness toward us in Christ Jesus (emphasis added).*
>
> —*Eph. 2:4–7*

These verses tell us we are seated *in* heaven, which is *in* Christ. We are currently seated there now, not one day. We are trees rooted in heaven. My roots don't run in the shallows of my circumstance, issues, or trials; they run deep within heaven, located within God Himself. Whatever is coming against me in this world is temporary. Every trial comes with an expiration date. We are stronger than the trial. Why? Because we are unshakable due to where we are located.

I love the perspective of heaven that C. S. Lewis provides in his book *The Great Divorce.*

> *Heaven is reality itself. All that is fully real is Heavenly. For all that can be shaken will be shaken and only the unshakeable remains.*[2]

What an amazing concept! Whatever is fully real is heavenly. I am a heavenly being created in the likeness of our heavenly God. When a circumstance arises, it will attempt to shake whatever it can. However, once I realize I am rooted in heaven, in Christ, I will not be influenced by the external.

Philippians 3 gives us this eye-opening truth.

For our citizenship is in heaven, from which also we eagerly wait for a Savior, the Lord Jesus Christ; who will transform the body of our humble state into conformity with the body of His glory, by the exertion of the power that He has even to subject all things to Himself.

—Phil. 3:20–21

There is a gem within this verse that can easily be overlooked. Paul is telling us that we are citizens of heaven and revealing what will happen to our physical bodies when Jesus returns for His bride, the believers. But there's more. Notice how Paul says "heaven, from which also we eagerly wait for a Savior." That is interesting. From where does he say we are waiting? From heaven, where are our citizenship is. We are waiting *from* heaven *for* Christ's return. The reality we walk in on earth is superseded by the reality of heaven. What is visible is not all that exists. There is so much more to take part in that we have yet to realize.

We are rooted in the rivers of heaven, yet the rivers remain unseen. I have all I need to thrive in every moment because I am pulling my nourishment from another world—God's world. Paul writes:

For momentary, light affliction is producing for us an eternal weight of glory far beyond all comparison, while we look not at the things which are seen, but at the things which are not seen; for the things which are seen are temporal, but the things which are not seen are eternal.

—2 Cor. 4:17–18

Here, we are told to focus on what is unseen in the midst of affliction. How are we supposed to focus on what we can't see? The answer, at the risk of sounding cliché, is faith. We walk by faith, not by sight (2 Cor. 5:7).

A Heavenly Transaction

So what is faith? Let's let God's word define it for us. "Now faith is the assurance of things hoped for, the conviction of things not seen" (Heb. 11:1). The word *conviction* can also be translated *evidence*. In essence, faith is the evidence that proves that whatever I am hoping for is on its way, even though I can't physically see it. It is the currency that allows us to make transactions from heaven to earth. With it, I can use the unseen resources of heaven in this present life.

I happen to believe that miracles still exist today. I am fully convinced that the impossible is possible for those who believe. I remember a moment before Holly and I were married when we were hanging out. For some reason, I requested that we go running. If you know anything about me, you know that if I have my heart set on something, it consumes me, and I will find a way to do it. For a reason I can't understand, running was my obsession that particular day. After I had presented my idea to Holly, she kindly said no and explained the reason.

Apparently, she had broken her ankle at a young age. At that time, her parents were unable to take her to the doctor and allowed time to heal her injury. So it was painful for her to wear high heels, run, or walk for long distances. Once I heard her story, faith rose up in me, and I said, "Then let's fix that!" I laid my hands on her, said a quick prayer, demanding the bones to be realigned and the pain to leave. As soon as I finished praying, I felt and heard her ankle pop underneath my hand. We were both surprised. "Did you hear that?" I asked. "Yes!" she exclaimed in excitement. "Then let's go test it out!"

We hurried out the door and began running around the neighborhood. She was able to make it all the way around the block without her ankle hurting at all. To this day, four years later, she has had no issues with her ankle. She is fully able to sport her high heels and walk long distances.

How is this possible? I pulled the resources of the unseen into the realm of the visible with the faith I had. I knew through reading the Bible that God is in the miracle business. When I discovered that, I gained the assurance to believe in miracles for my life as well. When faith is active, the problem doesn't seem so bad anymore, because I know the trial is trumped by a greater reality.

Faith is new vision, a supernatural set of eyes capable of piercing through the walls of the visible into the realm of the invisible. With faith, I can pray for the sick and see them recover. I can experience financial breakthroughs and see addictions broken. Anything becomes possible. Now hear me. I'm not suggesting that God is a genie that will grant all of our wishes. I am simply saying that there is more to life than what is logical and visible.

Childlike Trust

At its very root, faith is trust. Think of a child. Children are notorious for believing anything you tell them. When I was a kid, I was extremely gullible. I believed pretty much everything anyone said. This wasn't always helpful, however, because often the voices I listened to were unreliable sources. Because of that, I spent many years removing lies that were implanted at a young age. However, God's voice is extremely reliable. Everything He speaks is truth. It is impossible for a lie to pass through His lips. If I become like a gullible child who believes whatever the father speaks, then no matter what happens, His words will always be my reality. No storm will be too big, and no night will be too dark.

In Jeremiah 17, the prerequisite for strength in circumstances is trusting the Lord.

Blessed is the man who trusts in the LORD
And whose trust is the LORD.
For he will be like a tree planted by the water,
That extends its roots by a stream.

—*Jer. 17:7–8*

The birthplace of the tree of Jeremiah 17, the entire basis for this book, is trusting in the Lord. The key to thriving in trial is childlike trust. When I truly trust God, I am able to believe the best in any situation. So the question is, what do you believe? Do you believe what God says is true? Does that belief hold firm in contradicting moments? Have you become gullible for the word of God?

Praising in Prison

When we realize the beauty of the unseen and the eternal, the chaos of the visible and temporal will lose its bite. There is a powerful story in the book of Acts where Paul and Silas are thrown into prison. Before they found themselves in this predicament, they were doing what they were born for: spreading the gospel. On one journey, they were met by a slave girl who was a demon-possessed fortune teller. She followed the two around for days saying, "These men are bond-servants of the Most High God, who are proclaiming to you the way of salvation" (Acts 16:17). Even though she was correct, her words greatly annoyed Paul so much that he cast the demon out of her. That was great for the girl but not for her masters. They were furious that Paul ruined their stream of income, for they had been profiting from her satanic fortune-telling.

The angry bosses seized Paul and Silas, threw them before the authorities, and proceeded to accuse them of illegal activities. The crowd that had gathered for the event was convinced, tore off the apostles' clothes, and proceeded to beat them with rods. Shortly after, Paul and Silas were both thrown into prison with their feet fastened securely in stocks.

At that moment, most of us would be brought to tears, letting out our pain and anguish. But Paul and Silas are not recorded as doing such a thing. The Bible says they began to pray and sing hymns to God as the other prisoners listened. Something doesn't add up. They were just beaten severely and thrown into a nasty prison with their feet secured to the floor. That doesn't exactly sound like the ideal time to praise. They should have been contesting their arrests and fighting to get out.

Instead of looking at the mess they were in and complaining, they decided to praise. Praise is powerful. It allows us to step out of our visible circumstance and into the unseen reality of heaven's perfection. That's what Paul and Silas did. They remembered where they were rooted and praised from that place, seeing the pain of the situation but basking in the goodness of their God. In all of their hurt, they remained thankful.

Thankfulness is a lost art. Many people are continually complaining about what they don't have while devaluing what they do have. Truthfully, if I am not content with what I have now, I probably won't appreciate anything else I am given. Look around. Whatever is around you can be appreciated. When we remove the lens of familiarity and view all our possessions with a new set of eyes, thankfulness will bubble up quickly. The one who can't stop and enjoy where they are is so future-focused that they are completely calloused to the journey. The key is future expectation with current contentment. The two working together simultaneously create within us the ability to live life to the fullest.

In all moments, good or bad, easy or difficult, we are able to pull from the unseen. In that reality, we find every tool needed for every moment, remaining well-nourished through every season. A tree's unseen root system creates its visible appearance. Your roots run into heaven itself located smack-dab in the middle of the immovable God.

10

When Night Falls

This book would not be complete without acknowledging the fact of trials. It is wonderful when we can experience harmony of our surroundings and beliefs, but the world we live in is not that gracious. Eventually, we fall prey to negative circumstance, the dark and cloudy seasons. When night falls, we can seemingly lose our faith. Anyone can be happy when their surroundings are void of trial, but it takes a mature, confident believer to stand tall in the midst of negativity, keeping joy in their mind and peace in their soul. The maturing believer understands that circumstances aren't directly connected to the steering wheel of life. Their trust in God outweighs the size of their problem.

Trust beyond Trial

Straight out of high school, I enrolled in a trade school to learn the art of welding. My father was an experienced welder, and I had no other plans, so I figured I would follow in his footsteps. For two years, I received hands-on training on how to fuse two pieces of metal together. In class, we would often undergo what is called a bend test to show whether or not our welds were sturdy enough. After we had accomplished fusing two pieces of metal plates together, the instructors would cut out two strips from the finished plate. Those two strips would then be placed into a machine that would apply force and bend both strips. If the weld snapped, we failed. We passed only if our weld held strong through all the force that was applied. This is also true for believers. If the pressures of circumstance break us, it is evident that we didn't truly trust. Pressure reveals where our trust lies.

You know Jeremiah 17:7–8 well by now, or at least I hope you do. These verses make one promise: if we trust God, we can thrive through any external pressure. I'm not speaking of that clichéd, fear-based, I-hope-God-comes-through-for-me trust. Too often we pray for the best while expecting the worst and call it faith. I'm speaking of that immovable, internal assurance that God is who He says He is, the deep conviction that no matter what happens, everything will be all right. I have a friend who fits that description. I have seen him walk through some of the toughest seasons and situations imaginable while still clinging to the God he loves. No amount of external pressure is strong enough to break his beliefs.

If you back up a couple of verses in Jeremiah 17, you can catch a glimpse of the alternative outcome of those who choose to trust in something other than God.

> *Cursed is the man who trusts in mankind*
> *And makes flesh his strength,*
> *And whose heart turns away from the LORD.*
> *For he will be like a bush in the desert*
> *And will not see when prosperity comes,*
> *But will live in stony wastes in the wilderness,*
> *A land of salt without inhabitant.*
>
> —*Jer. 17:5–6*

These are not the most exciting couple of verses, but that does not take away the powerful truth they reveal. Here, God isn't threatening to curse us. He is stating the inevitable outcome for those who choose the wrong source on which to lean. When people or possessions are our go-to, we no longer live as thriving trees but stay stuck like bushes in the dessert, desperately crying out for nourishment, much like the wandering Israelites. We see it all over the world, people giving others shoes to fill that they soon discover were never the right fit. I can think of many times, in hard moments, that I trusted something or someone to be my source. Eventually, they all let me down. Every time. Of course, that is not because people are evil. It is because they were never meant to carry the load of our faith. I'm not saying we shouldn't trust people. I am simply saying that there is only one who was built to carry our burdens, and He is willing and ready.

God will never let you down. It's not in His nature. When I truly believe that He is for me, not against me, and that He has my best interests in mind, trusting becomes easy. God is extending an invitation to each of us to step into His world where the currency is pure faith. The question is, what do you believe about God in hard times? Do your beliefs seem to differ according to your current situation?

The Beauty of a Trial

Trials do not change our beliefs; they reveal them. Anyone can seemingly have faith when life doesn't require it. What is often perceived as faith is actually good observation. It's easy to say God is good when everything in life is good. But what about when everything falls apart? Does your faith stop when good times cease? If so, it becomes evident that you never understood or experienced true faith in the first place. C. S. Lewis, in his book *A Grief Observed*, called this particular faith a house of cards—something that appears sturdy but is easily toppled.

I've got nothing that I hadn't bargained for. Of course it is different when the thing happens to oneself, not to others, and in reality, not in imagination. Yes; but should it, for a sane man, make quite such a difference as this? No. And it wouldn't for a man whose faith had been real faith and whose concern for other people's sorrows had been real concern. The case is too plain. If my house has collapsed at one blow, that is because it was a house of cards. The faith which 'took these things into account' was not faith but imagination.[1]

Lewis discovered that faith moved by wind is not faith at all. It is a flimsy structure, disguised as trust. The beauty of a trial is that it reveals true beliefs. Beliefs are not conditional. They do not change with circumstances. Good times can potentially mask true beliefs, giving the appearance of faith, whereas hard times actually reveal them.

When my son got sick at an early stage in his life, what I truly believed leaked out. Before that, I was confident in God as the healer, 100 percent of the time. It was easy to give advice to those in the midst of sickness. I stood on the truth of the word and spoke to them accordingly. I truly thought I believed in healing wholeheartedly and that sickness didn't have to exist in the body of a believer—until it happened to me. When my son became ill and my prayers seemed to be missing their target, I began to question the healing business. The circumstance began to change what I believed. Or so I thought. It is evident now that this particular trial didn't modify my beliefs but exposed cracks in their foundation. Though the illness my son experienced wasn't anything close to life-threatening, it still had the ability to bring me to a place of doubt. He was soon completely healed and back to his joyful self. But in this brief moment when my faith faced off with the enemy's attacks, I clearly saw what had been hidden before.

James 1:2–3 says, "Consider it all joy, my brethren, when you encounter various trials, knowing that the testing of your faith produces endurance." How is that possible? Because trials expose what our faith is made of. The true test of faith is a contradicting trial. There is, in a sense, a beauty to be witnessed in a trial. In that moment, either beliefs are reinforced or lies are exposed. Peter writes this:

> *In this you greatly rejoice, even though now for a little while, if necessary, you have been distressed by various trials, so that the proof of your faith, being more precious than gold which is perishable, even though tested by fire, may be found to result in praise and glory and honor at the revelation of Jesus Christ; and though you have not seen Him, you love Him, and though you do not see Him now, but believe in Him, you greatly rejoice with joy inexpressible and full of glory.*
>
> *—1 Pet. 1:6–8*

According to Peter, when your faith in God is pure, the outcome of your trial will result in pure praise. However, this only comes when you have a revelation of the nature of Jesus. In other words, when I know who He is, my love and admiration for Him can't be consumed, even by the fires of trial.

Your faith can only be tested through contradicting circumstance. I wish it wasn't so. I wish our faith could be tested in peaceful seasons. The truth is, the durability of your faith can only be revealed in a storm.

Sleeping through the Storm

In Matthew 8, there is the well-known story of when Jesus calmed a storm. Up until recently, my focus had always been on the action Jesus took to bring peace to the chaos. But now, I see something new in this story. Obviously, what He did was truly remarkable and supernatural. It shows the authority of Jesus and the lack of power of the enemy. This is good news! However, I recently noticed something I had never realized before when my pastor Barry Tubbs Jr. was preaching from these verses:

And when He got into the boat, His disciples followed Him. And behold, there arose a great storm on the sea, so that the boat was being covered with the waves; but Jesus Himself was asleep. And they came to Him and woke Him, saying, "Save us, Lord; we are perishing!" He said to them, "Why are you afraid, you men of little faith?" Then he got up and rebuked the winds and the sea, and it became perfectly calm. The men were amazed and said, "What kind of a man is this, that even winds and sea obey Him?"

—Matt. 8:23–27

It is interesting that the Bible says Jesus was asleep. The waves and the winds were beating against the place where Jesus was resting His head, yet He was still able to stay in a place of deep serenity. Was He just a heavy sleeper? I don't think so. He knew where He was going because the father had told Him. When you know your destination, peace remains constant. While Jesus was enjoying a time of regeneration, His disciples were on the deck freaking out. These experienced fishermen were witnessing a storm, firsthand, that they didn't know how to navigate. So they did what they knew to do. Get Jesus!

Interestingly enough the storm didn't wake Jesus up; the disciples did. Do you think they were doing Him a favor? If they hadn't awakened Him, would this story have ended with our savior at the bottom of the sea? I personally believe that He was asleep because He knew nothing could actually end His life unless He willingly gave it up. The only reason He died on the cross was because He chose it. Bill Johnson says, "You only have authority over the storm you can sleep in."[2] Jesus realized His authority, and because of that, He was able to keep peace in situations void of peace.

After Jesus was awakened by His fearful followers, notice that He said, "Why are you afraid, you men of little faith?" In other words, don't you trust God? Then, He calmed the storm. I have always believed that the purpose of this story is only to reveal the powerful works of Jesus. While it does reveal His power, I believe there is an underlying message that has been missed. I would like to submit that Jesus never wanted to rebuke the waves. He only did so due to the fear the disciples had. When Jesus awoke, His first words were "Why are you afraid?" The implication is that this current storm, though large, was not something that should have produced fear in these men of faith. It was not a disaster that could harm them.

Jesus's resting in the chaos is evidence that the storm they encountered was not one that could pull them under. If the disciples had looked at the current state of the Messiah rather than the state of the storm, they could have joined Him in a nap. But instead, they let the appearance of danger get the best of them. So often, we go through difficult situations and expect Jesus to make them vanish. But the truth is, your boat was built to withstand the storm. I have never been big on storms. Even as I type this chapter, a loud storm rages right outside my window. It humors me that the revelation we receive is often immediately put to the test.

Don't misunderstand me. I am not demeaning the authority Jesus walked in. Neither am I demeaning the authority that we walk in. Jesus gave us the same authority that He walked in so we would use it against the powers of darkness. But often we spend too much time trying to rebuke the winds around us when we could be resting with Jesus. There is a time to rebuke, and there is a time to rest. The simplest way to decipher the right direction is to look at Jesus. What is He doing during your storm?

In John 5:19, Jesus said, "Truly, truly, I say to you, the Son can do nothing of Himself, unless it is something He sees the Father doing; for whatever the Father does, these things the Son also does in like manner." Jesus had the kind of relationship with his father that allowed Him to see what His father was doing in every situation. If His father wasn't doing it, Jesus didn't do it. Jesus was asleep in the boat because He saw His father sleeping. I believe that Jesus is calling us to that same level of connection with Him. What is Jesus doing during your trial? Are you doing what you see Him doing, or are you blindly doing what your tradition teaches?

Our ability to thrive in all circumstances is truly contingent on our connection with Jesus. We are in union with Him. He is with us at all times. We have unlimited access to His voice. We are not left to make independent decisions in this life; rather, we are invited to let Him lead us through the beautiful sound of His voice.

A Supernatural Support System

If you have a background in church, you are probably familiar with the story of Jesus walking on water found in Matthew 14. Before we dive into the moment when Jesus defied physics, let's back up to see the context. John the Baptist had just been beheaded in prison. When Jesus heard this, He attempted to seclude Himself by taking a boat to a private place. I assume He needed some alone time with His father to mourn the loss of a friend and receive peace. Here, Jesus shows a practical tool for dealing with loss: get the father's perspective first. Many times, our faith takes a step back in seasons of loss, simply because we listened to the wrong words from the wrong voice. Jesus was then rudely interrupted by a crowd of people who were earnestly seeking His life-giving presence. With compassion in His heart, He healed all those who were sick among them.

As night began to fall, the disciples asked to send the crowds away. After all, they were hungry, and there was no food to be found. The only food they had available was five loaves of bread and two fish. Obviously, that was well under the amount needed to feed thousands of people—or so the disciples thought. Jesus took the small portion, blessed it, and began to distribute it to the disciples and the crowd. When it was all over and each person had their fill, they gathered the leftovers, filling 12 baskets. Another miracle had just been witnessed, and the disciples once again found themselves in awe of this man.

Jesus then decided to send His disciples on a boat to go to another city while He sent away the people. As the boat drifted out, a storm rolled in that began to beat against their tiny boat. At this point, the disciples were more than likely finding it difficult to remain calm. As the storm progressed, a shadowy figure was seen standing on the surface of the sea. With fear in their voices, the men in the beaten boat cried out, "It is a ghost!" (Matt. 14:26). Jesus called to them, saying, "It is I; do not be afraid" (Matt. 14:27). Without hearing a name, Peter recognized His voice. The voice he had come to know well was now calling out from the dark.

Peter's next statement seems odd. "Lord, if it is You, command me to come to You on the water" (Matt. 14:28). Then Jesus shouted one powerful word: "Come!" (Matt. 14:29). The fact that Peter started his sentence with *Lord* tells me he knew who was speaking. Why, then, did he ask for a command to step out onto the sea? Why did he need Jesus to say "Come"?

Peter's very first interaction with Jesus is found in Matthew 4. He and his brother Andrew were doing what they did best: catching fish. The next thing they knew, a random man approached them saying, "Follow Me, and I will make you fishers of men" (Matt. 4:19)—or in today's language, "Let's go fish for some people!" I'm sure Peter and Andrew were no strangers to crazy people with requests, but something was different about this man. His words were glowing with life and purpose. Something came alive in them that demanded embarking on an unknown journey. Immediately, they dropped what they knew and followed who they didn't. Fast forward to a moment when Peter is once again in a boat staring out into the unknown.

In the midst of a storm, Peter remembered the voice that called him out in the beginning. All he needed in this moment was a command to come again. Once he heard it, thinking went out the window, and faith came alive inside. The storm didn't matter, the boat didn't matter, and the sea under him didn't matter. He stepped out into the impossible with full assurance that Jesus wouldn't let him down. Childlike trust was witnessed by all watching. The one he trusted most in the world just gave him an impossible command that he wasn't about to ignore. Faith does that to you. It causes you to dismiss all logical decisions and blindly act. What you physically see is no longer the deciding factor, because you know deep within that anything is possible. So there was Peter, walking on the sea, with eyes locked on Jesus. The very thing he once made a living from was now under his feet.

Today, the same voice that called you in the beginning is still calling out to you saying, "Come join me in the impossible." So faith comes from hearing, and hearing by the word of Christ (Rom. 10:17). When God speaks, my ears open. When my ears open, I can recognize His voice. When I recognize His voice, I can believe what He speaks. Once we hear His voice, nothing is impossible for us. He is not asking us to stay in the boat of fear as circumstances beat us to death. He is inviting us into the eye of the storm to experience supernatural peace. You were created to thrive in all circumstances because the king is always with you. In the brightest light and in the darkest night, He is right there by your side.

Sadly, things didn't end well for Peter in this story. His downfall wasn't due to the harsh environment, but instead to a shift in focus. How true that is! Our shortcomings aren't due to the trials we experience; they are due to our wrong perception. Faith always sees past the visible problem and believes in the solution: God Himself. For just a moment, Peter moved his focus from the savior to the storm and in doing so began to sink into his physical circumstance. What can we learn from Peter's fall? Don't break focus with Jesus. When we look away from the king, we become susceptible to whatever the enemy throws at us.

I love what my pastor once said about this story, that Peter wasn't walking on the water but was walking on the word. The supernatural support system holding Peter above the water was the command from Jesus to come. That tells me this: what God speaks to you will support you through anything. When Peter changed his focal point, he forgot for a second what Jesus said, thereby removing himself from the structure Jesus provided. Never lose sight of the word you have from God. It is that word from Him that will replay over and over in your mind, drowning out the noise of the enemy around you. If Jesus says "Come," He isn't lying. It is time to trust Him.

The Enemy's Plan of Confusion

I said earlier that trials don't change our beliefs; they expose them. Although that is true, there is one exception. There are times when the enemy plants thoughts in our minds that cause us to embrace a belief that isn't actually ours. He is, after all, the author of confusion.

Napoleon Hill, author of *Outwitting the Devil*, claims to have documented a conversation he had with the devil. Whether its content was metaphorical or literal, I do not know. However, there are some interesting parts, particularly this one, where the devil is explaining what a drifter is:

> *A drifter is one who accepts whatever life throws in his way without making a protest or putting up a fight. He doesn't know what he wants from life and spends all his time getting just that. A drifter has lots of opinions but they are not his own. Most of them are supplied by me.[3]*

More often than we realize, Satan, by whatever means necessary, is attempting to plant beliefs that don't actually belong to us in hopes that we will take them and care for them as our own. As Hill said, many people's opinions are supplied by Satan. I can think of times when a negative circumstance happened in my life, causing me to move from beliefs of faith to something else completely. It wasn't what I truly believed, but something I claimed anyway. Though trials reveal true beliefs, they also reveal counterfeit ones.

We see the biblical example of this in Mark 9 where Jesus healed a demon-possessed boy. In this story, the boy's father had already attempted to bring him to Jesus's disciples to receive healing. However, they were unsuccessful in their efforts. Jesus then finds a crowd gathered around His disciples and an open argument in progress. When he discovers that his followers failed to cast out this demon, He verbally expresses His annoyance with their actions. "O unbelieving generation, how long shall I be with you? How long shall I put up with you? Bring him to Me!" (Mark 9:19). Now it was Jesus's turn to show them how it's done. After a short dialog between Jesus and the boy's father, the father begs Jesus to heal his son "*if* you can" (Mark 9:22). Apparently, our Messiah was surprised by this response. He exclaimed, "If you can? All things are possible to him who believes" (Mark 9:23). Then the boy's father gives an odd response: "I do believe; help my unbelief" (Mark 9:24). The story then ends with Jesus casting out the unclean spirit and restoring the boy's sanity.

This boy's father gives us a glimpse of the enemy's tactic. Even though we are standing with Jesus, fully believing He can do all things, it is still possible to be tempted with the enemy's thoughts. If we identify with them, he wins. But there is good news in this story. Jesus will help us remove the thoughts that aren't ours. How? Through His word. If you remember, in Chapter 3 of this book, we discussed the pruning process of God in the mind of the believer. He is constantly at work snipping off those wrong thoughts and restoring truths. Don't identify with the enemy's lies. Remember what your father has said about you and to you.

The Visible Side of Faith

Faith is all about believing in what is unseen, giving us hope in all circumstances. Sadly, many people think that having faith will keep them out of hard times. While this is a wonderful idea, it happens to be false. Faith doesn't exempt you from trials, but it does change the way you respond to them. If you want to know the depth of someone's faith, watch how they respond in tough situations.

James writes in his letter, "But someone may well say, 'You have faith and I have works; show me your faith without the works, and I will show you my faith by my works" (James 2:18). James makes it plain; there is a visible side of faith. Someone who says they have faith but no observable action to back it up is merely someone who is all talk without real trust. When I genuinely trust God, I refrain from running when trials or tragedies hit and stand firm on the truth I already know about Him. The key is not mustering up faith on your own; it's seeing Him for who He truly is and allowing Him to fill you with His faith.

Christians shouldn't be looked at as a group of people without problems. If you became a Christian because you were promised an easy life void of issues, I'm sorry, but someone lied to you. We will always encounter issues because we currently walk in this fallen world. But I promise you this. Christians have everything they need to rise above anything and everything. There is always a heavenly solution to an earthly problem. When you discover the greatness of your God, you will realize the insignificance of your issue.

You are the light of the world. A city set on a hill cannot be hidden; nor does anyone light a lamp and put it under a basket, but on the lampstand, and it gives light to all who are in the house. Let your light shine before men in such a way that they may see your good works, and glorify your Father who is in heaven.

—Matt. 5:14–16

Jesus says we are the light of the world—not someday, but right now. It's our nature as believers to shine brightly. Kris Vallotton, a pastor at Bethel Church in Redding, California, once said in a message that people don't go onto the light to stare at the light; they go into the light to see. The goal of believers is not to have all eyes on them; it is so all eyes will be on Jesus. We are not *in* the spotlight so others can see how spiritual we are; we *are* the spotlight that points directly to the power source, God Himself. When unbelievers approach us, we have the wonderful privilege to illuminate their perspective through the light of our lives. When we live as light, other people are exposed to the reality of the kingdom and the goodness of God. The blinders come off, the veil is removed, and they can clearly see the true nature of reality.

Matthew 5:16 says, "Let your light shine before men in such a way that they may see your good works, and glorify your Father who is in heaven." That tells me one important thing: our works show our faith. When I live as light, everything I do proves to others that my faith is more than words. But not only are they up to speed with what I believe, it rubs off on them, compelling them to worship the God I portrayed through my actions. My life then becomes contagious worship to all I encounter. Do you want to change the world? Then show them who you are. Step into the night and shine your light.

Remember, in this life, you represent God. The world has an opportunity to see the power of the gospel in the lives of believers. You are a being of hope because the God of hope dwells within you. You have become a model for the power of God. You are not a victim. You already have what it takes to thrive in this world. Now recognize it and put it on display for all the world to see.

Conclusion

There is one life-changing reality that I have aimed to impart through each page of this book: the Christian life has no limits. My intentions for this book were not to create a new formula for reaching success but to awaken the reader to a greater reality—the reality of identity. When people discover who they are and who He is, they naturally rise to a higher level of living. This book has provided a few practical tools to use in life such as prayer and praise, but I pray that you do not confine yourself to any new formulas. My hope is that you have been enlightened to a new world and that you will allow the Holy Spirit to lead you through this new understanding.

We were born to thrive in every area of life. No matter the circumstance, no matter the problem, Christians are planted to stand above the rest. Being fully rooted by fully trusting, we are to be a monument of His majesty in this world. If we are doomed to live life and respond to world issues like the rest of humankind, then following Jesus has no observable effect on humanity. However, when Jesus becomes my savior, I am not only re-created in spirit but also in my walk. When I discover all He has made possible in me, I can no longer be satisfied living in mediocrity. I am then pushed into victorious beliefs that catapult me into fearless living.

The journey becomes a lot easier to navigate when I discover that He has already given me all I need to succeed.

Grace and peace be multiplied to you in the knowledge of God and of Jesus our Lord; seeing that His divine power has granted to us everything pertaining to life and godliness, through the true knowledge of Him who called us by His own glory and excellence.

—2 Pet. 1:2–3

Peter tells us, by the inspiration of the Holy Spirit, that everything we need for this life is already within us. Why? Because the king is in us. Where the king is, there is His kingdom. I am no longer required to run to the next best thing to receive what I need because He has given me all I need in Him. I can look well-nourished and walk godly today. Let's return one final time to the verses that started this journey.

Blessed is the man who trusts in the LORD
And whose trust is the LORD.
For he will be like a tree planted by the water,
That extends its roots by a stream
And will not fear when the heat comes;
But its leaves will be green,
And it will not be anxious in a year of drought
Nor cease to yield fruit.

—Jer. 17:7–8

Let these words sink in. Return to them often. If at any moment your walk begins to reflect decay, you have forgotten who you truly are. Return to His words and let them wash off every wrong belief you picked up on your journey. As a Christian, you truly are a mighty tree of God with roots that run deep into the supernatural rivers of heaven that allow you thrive in every aspect of life!

Notes

Think Like an Evergreen

1. Abraham Lincoln, "The Emancipation Proclamation," January 1, 1863, *HistoryNet*, accessed February 28, 2018, http://www.historynet.com/emancipation-proclamation-text.

The Journey of Maturity

1. *Thayer's Greek-English Lexicon of the New Testament* (Grand Rapids, MI: Zondervan Publishing House, 1965), 38.

Connected Conversation

1. Anne Lamott, *Traveling Mercies: Some Thoughts on Faith* (New York: Anchor Books, 1999), 134.

2. *Thayer's Greek-English Lexicon of the New Testament*, 432.

Inside the Unseen

1. John Gill, *Exposition of the Entire Bible*, quoted in *Bible Study Tools*, accessed March 3, 2018, https://www.biblestudytools.com/commentaries/gills-exposition-of-the-bible/1-kings-8-27.html.

2. C.S. Lewis, *The Great Divorce* (New York: HarperCollins, 2001), 70–71.

When Night Falls

1. C.S. Lewis, *A Grief Observed* (New York: HarperCollins, 1994), 36–37.

2. Bill Johnson, *Bill Johnson Ministries*, accessed March 4, 2018, https://www.facebook.com/BillJohnsonMinistries/posts/10150273208133387.

3. Napoleon Hill, *Outwitting the Devil* (New York: Sterling Publishing, 2011), 73.

Visit www.stevenneilwalker.com to see the latest content, including videos, blog posts, and book updates. You can also subscribe to Steven's mailing list!

Catch up with Steven over the following channels:

Facebook: @stevenneilwalker
Instagram: @steven_n_walker
Twitter: @_steven_walker
Email: stevenwalker@ilovetheway.tv

The Way Church
"Discover Your Good Life"

Come by and visit! We would love to meet you.
Check out our website to see what we're all about!

4332 East Highway 377, Granbury, Texas 76049
www.ilovetheway.tv

CPSIA information can be obtained
at www.ICGtesting.com
Printed in the USA
LVHW091650071120
671040LV00014B/50

9 781632 962164